CISTERCIAN FATHERS SERIES: NUMBER TWENTY-TWO

Aelred of Rievaulx

DIALOGUE ON THE SOUL

CISTERCIAN FATHERS SERIES: NUMBER TWENTY-TWO

Aelred of Rievaulx

DIALOGUE ON THE SOUL

Translated, with an Introduction, by
C. H. TALBOT

§

Cistercian Publications
Kalamazoo, Michigan
1981

CISTERCIAN FATHERS SERIES

Dialogue On The Soul is a translation of the *De anima* of Aelred of Rievaulx (1109–1166). The Latin text used was prepared by C. H. Talbot and published first in *Aelred of Rievaulx: De Anima, Mediaeval and Renaissance Studies, Supplement I,* by the Warburg Institute, The University of London (1952), and subsequently in A. Hoste and C. H. Talbot, edd., *Aelredi Rievallensis Opera Omnia I: Opera Ascetica, Corpus Christianorum, Continuatio Medievalis,* 1, by Brepols of Turnholt, Belgium (1971).

Library of Congress Cataloging in Publication Data:

Ethelred, Saint, 1109?-1166.
   Dialogue on the soul.

   (Cistercian Fathers series ; no. 22)
   Translation of De anima.
   Bibliography: p.
   Includes index.
   1. Soul—Early works to 1800.   I. Title.
BT740.E813   1981   233'.5   80-19699
ISBN 0-87907-222-9

CONTENTS

*J*T IS NOW almost thirty years since I first published Aelred's *De anima* in the series *Mediaeval and Renaissance Studies,* published by the Warburg Institute, University of London. Surprisingly, the views expressed then in the Introduction appear to need no modification and in consequence I have had no compunction in repeating them, though here and there a few additions have been made to the bibliography.

In the notes to the text the *Patrologia Latina* of Migne has been used throughout. This had been done for the sake of consistency as well as for convenience. New editions of certain authors have been published in recent years, notably of Saint Bernard of Clairvaux, but judging by my own experience I am inclined to believe that not all libraries or institutions go to the trouble of acquiring them when they have a perfectly serviceable text on their shelves. I have, accordingly, used Migne. In the original edition of *De anima* the actual words, apart from the references, were quoted from various authors in order to show how dependent Aelred's text was on the sources he employed. In the translation this procedure has not been considered necessary. One hopes that readers will not feel deprived.

C. H. T.

London, 1980

3

INTRODUCTION

ELRED OF RIEVAULX, the author of *De anima*, was born in Hexham of a family whose connections with the Church stretched far back into the Northumbrian past.[1] His great-grandfather had been sacrist of Durham Cathedral, his grandfather had been treasurer there, whilst his father, Eilaf, was hereditary priest of Hexham. All these members of his family had been forced in turn to surrender their positions as a result of the reforming movements that swept through the north of England. It was only to be expected that this awakened in him a consciousness of the new spirit that was rejuvenating ecclesiastical life and it is not surprising that, later, he was to associate himself with the most uncompromising reformers of monastic tradition.

Though his father had lost his rights over the Priory of Hexham, he still retained his influence as a landed proprietor, and it was probably in this capacity that he was able to bring to the notice of the King of Scotland the suitability of his son, Aelred, to be companion to the King's sons, Henry and Waldef.[2] At the court, Aelred's qualities soon made him a general favourite and the King thought so highly of his character that he intended to promote him to the most important ecclesiastical preferment in the realm.[3] All these plans were frustrated when, during a royal mission to the Archbishop of York in 1134, Aelred made a detour to visit Walter d'Espec, the founder of the cistercian abbey of Rievaulx.[4] Listening to the enthusiastic description of cistercian life and its ideals, Aelred was fired with a determination to forsake secular ambitions and to devote himself to the pursuit of spiritual perfection.

Aelred's experiences as a novice in the somewhat grim environment of cistercian life are charmingly described in the opening chapters of the *Speculum charitatis.*[5] They brought out his finest qualities, which, allied to his distinguished bearing and his exceptional gifts of mind, marked him out as one destined to exercise a powerful influence over his associates. Soon, his quick grasp of affairs, his administrative ability and his consummate prudence gained the confidence of his abbot and, after being sent to Rome in 1142 to represent the Cistercians on the question of the disputed election at York,[6] he was appointed Master of Novices. In this post his sympathetic nature, his tolerance, and his deep psychological insight found free expression. The pages of the *Speculum charitatis,* which Saint Bernard had encouraged him to write, show with what earnestness, delicacy, and tact he moulded his young charges to the ideals of the benedictine rule; and his success in tempering their weaknesses and inuring them to the severity of cistercian regulations indicated that he was admirably equipped to govern a community. Consequently, when the Earl of Lincoln offered to establish a cistercian monastery at Revesby, Aelred was unanimously elected to be its first superior.[7]

During the next five years he succeeded not merely in establishing the material prosperity of his house and the steady growth in numbers of the community, but also in impressing his personality on the clergy and people of the Lincoln diocese. The recent disturbances in the county had reduced the region to a waste and moral standards had sunk to the lowest level.[8] Aelred's sermons at the local synods did much to raise the standards both of clergy and people, and as a result his reputation was considerably enhanced.

When the resignation of Maurice left Rievaulx without an abbot, Aelred's success at Revesby weighed heavily in his favour, and he was duly elected superior in 1147. From remarks made by his biographer, Walter Daniel, it would appear that the community at Rievaulx had, under Maurice, increased too quickly and through indiscriminate recruitment had accepted many who were ill-suited to the rigours of cistercian life. As a result, the monastery was disturbed from time to time by internal discord. By patience and tolerance Aelred was able to smooth out these passing troubles. He never tired of repeating that the supreme and singular glory of Rievaulx was that it had learnt, better than all other monastic houses, to bear with the weak and to have compassion on those in need.[9] This spirit of mildness and benevolence attracted many who found themselves unable to settle where the Rule was applied with rigour and severity, and as a result the community, which in 1132 may have numbered twenty-five members, grew rapidly to three hundred by 1142[10] and to six hundred and forty by 1165.[11] Though this extraordinary expansion might have been fraught with great danger under any ordinary government, under Aelred the original discipline and fervour of the Order were maintained.

This was accomplished in spite of the heavy responsibilities that lay upon him for supervising the welfare of Rievaulx's many filiations, for attending the annual General Chapters at Cîteaux,[12] for preaching at synods and for dealing with the multifarious duties connected with his position as a noted public figure. The three hundred letters, now lost, addressed to kings, nobles, archbishops, bishops, and other people of importance attest his involvement in affairs that were far removed from his cares as abbot.[13] He never forgot, however, that he was the father of a community and it was to its members that he directed all his affection and his energy. Apart from the sermons which he was obliged to deliver to the community on special feasts, he wrote for his monks several small treatises; the *De anima,* penned during his final illness, was one of these.

Most of Aelred's works were written when his health was already undermined by arthritis. But in spite of the constant attacks of pain which left him prostrate and oftentimes

speechless, his pages are pervaded by such calm and serenity
that one might think they had been penned by a man
untroubled by the harsh realities of life. During his closing
years he was allowed by special dispensation of the General
Chapter of the Order to live apart in a small hut adjoining
the infirmary. There, wracked by pain, frail and twisted like a
piece of parchment,[14] he would crouch by the fire, reading
over and over again the *Confessions* of Saint Augustine, or,
when he was free from pain, he would discuss with the
monks who crowded into his cell the questions that arose
during the course of their studies.[15]

It is not without significance that the *De anima* is written
in the form of a dialogue and it may be that this reflects in
some way one of the discussions held in his cell during his
final illness. Two verses at the end seem to imply that the
treatise was cut short by the death of the author, but a careful examination of the concluding paragraphs and the
undoubted climax to which they lead suggest that Aelred had
already completed his task when, on 11 January 1167, whilst
the narrative of the Passion was being read out to him, he
rendered his soul to God.[16]

The appearance in the early days of the cistercian Order
of several treatises on the nature of the soul indicates a certain preoccupation with this fundamental problem of psychology. But it is doubtful whether the Cistercians were
concerned with the purely theoretical aspects of the question, since philosophical speculation was not encouraged. It
seems more likely that these treatises were intended to promote an interest in spiritual and mystical matters. The possibility of basing a complete system of spiritual *askesis* on the
recognition of the soul's resemblance to God had been
adumbrated by early christian writers.[17] Saint Gregory of
Nyssa had understood and explained that the human soul
bore in its simplicity, immortality, and other qualities a

strong reflection of the image of God.[18] But, like other theologians of the same period, he had stopped short at a description of the mere external manifestation of this resemblance. Saint Augustine provided a more developed doctrine in the *De Trinitate,* and it was by grafting his profound psychological analysis on to the original concept of the image that the twelfth century writers produced a rounded synthesis.

An outline of their teaching, prescinding from individual differences of interpretation and emphasis, may be summed up as follows:

Since God is ineffable, any knowledge of the divine nature must come to man not directly but indirectly through the imprints he perceives of it in creation. This derivative and relative apprehension leaves the inner life of God as complete a mystery as before. The inability to understand, much less to explain, the nature of God is comprehensible when man has to admit that he cannot explain the functioning of his own body and much less the operation of his own soul. But by contemplating his own human nature it may be possible to perceive some faint glimmering of what God really is. He sees that the soul vivifies every member of his body and exercises in the body a power analogous to that which God exercises in the universe. And as the soul is present in every part of the body and not less in the part than in the whole, the inference is that God also is one, simple, indivisible Being, sustaining and animating every atom of the universe. So, man becomes aware of God's omnipresence. Yet, though man is conscious of the all-pervading power of his own soul, the mode of its presence in the body escapes him. The soul, therefore, is to some degree incomprehensible and it shares in the incomprehensibility of God. And since the soul is one and indivisible, possessing no parts which can disintegrate, and always remains what and as it is, it resembles the everlasting Being and shares in some manner in his immortality.

The closest resemblance of the soul to God, however, lies in the analogy of the three faculties, intellect, memory, and will, to the three Persons of the Trinity; for, as the existence of the memory connotes the co-existence of the intellect and the will, so the existence of God the Father connotes the co-existence of the Son and Holy Spirit; and as the operations of the faculties are inseparable and indivisible, so also the operations of the Trinity are inseparable and indivisible. If Adam had made the right use of these three faculties, man's resemblance to God would have remained unimpaired: the pursuit of truth and goodness would have followed the natural exercise of his spiritual powers. But the acceptance of error in place of truth and the choice of evil instead of good led to the destruction of man's initial happiness. The misguided use of the intellect and the perverse exercise of the will had as its dire consequence the expulsion from paradise and the sojourn in a hostile world. As a result, man found himself in a 'region of dissimilitude'[19] where the original likeness to God was distorted and the pursuit of truth was painful. Man's perpetual problem lies in finding the means to regain his former state of bliss.

To restore man to his lost estate is the object of the ascetic life. It consists in a concentration of the three highest faculties of the soul, memory, intellect, and will, on their highest possible object, God. By a study of and a spiritual assimilation to the Trinity the soul will take on its erstwhile resemblance and, instead of remaining a mere caricature of the noble being it once was, it will become its perfect self; for its perfection consists in remembering without forgetfulness, knowing without error, and loving without satiety. In reaching for the unchangeable good, the soul with its faculties will become stabilised in good, will become transformed, will become deiform. As Saint Bernard said: *Sic affici, deificari est.*

Such is the doctrine to which Aelred's *De anima* is

attached. It is a doctrine which had the widest repercussions. It dominated the teaching of the early Cistercians and through them, particularly through Saint Bernard, it penetrated the writings of Eckhart, Gerlac Peters, Thomas à Kempis and the Brethren of the Common Life at Windesheim. Not all of these ideas are fully developed in Aelred's *De anima,* but those that are omitted find their place in other works of his, specifically in the *Speculum charitatis.*

A SUMMARY OF THE DIALOGUE

Book I deals with the fundamental questions concerning the nature of the soul—its simplicity, immateriality, immortality, and substantial unity. The starting point of the discussion arises from the assertion made by Plotinus that the soul is not contained within the body, but contains it. The soul endows the body with substantial existence, and since it is made to the image of God, who is essentially omnipresent in all creation, it vivifies all the bodily members, suffering no diminution or contraction through mutilation or corruption of the body. It is a simple, not a composite, reality. A negative definition would say that it is independent of the four primeval elements, earth, air, fire, and water; but in positive terms it is differentiated from animals, angelic spirits, and God. Essentially it is rational life. But what is life? Is it a substance or an accident? The answer is that life (to borrow a platonic phrase) is a kinetic power. It is not, except in the wide metaphorical sense, a spirit, but a subtle, internal force giving movement to corporeal elements and expressing itself under various guises in plants, animals, and the bodily senses. In animals the life force is little more than an airy and fiery quality, incorporeal in comparison with the lower elements of earth and water, but corporeal in comparison with the rational spirit of man. What distinguishes the soul of man from the souls of plants and animals, and makes it superior to both, is the faculty of reason.

Reason can act independently of the senses and can turn back upon itself, a fact that proves both its simplicity and its immateriality. But reason cannot be separated in its operation from the two other spiritual faculties, memory and will. Accordingly, it must exist along with these powers in the soul or constitute the soul itself. Were these three powers present in the soul as parts in a whole or as accidents in a subject, they might possibly be separated. But since it is impossible to conceive of the soul being deprived of reason, memory, or will, they must form its very substance.

The main function of the soul in the body, besides the exercise of the three superior faculties, is to vivify, nourish, and propagate the body; but though these are three distinct and different functions, they do not connote the existence of three or even two souls. One rational soul fulfils all these functions.

How then are the two opposite principles, material and immaterial, united? The answer is that there is a subtle medium, *sensus,* half-corporeal, half-spiritual, which through its kinship with both principles is able to act as a kind of amalgam and mould them into perfect unity. What the origin is of this spirit entity, the soul, is not clear, but Augustine's solution to the problem is considered, for various reasons, to provide the safest answer.

Book II deals with memory, reason, and will. It opens with the question of memory. It is evident that the word signifies much more than the modern psychological content of the term. In Aelred, as in Augustine, it applies not merely to remembrance of the past but to everything that is present in the soul without its being explicitly known or perceived. The modern terms equivalent to this *memoria* would be the unconscious or subconscious, provided such terms were enlarged to include, besides the presence of states not actually perceived, the metaphysical presence of God.

Memory is primarily the storehouse of images received through the senses. But how does an incorporeal faculty contain and conserve the images of corporeal objects? The answer is that, on the analogy of a mirror that reflects images greater than itself, the memory is spiritually, not materially, greater than any corporeal image or object, and that it can therefore grasp them in a manner totally different from that in which they exist. The abstract laws of science and art are also lodged in the memory, and this fact proves not only the memory's incorporeity, but also its power to hold innate ideas. Animals, too, possess memory, but with them it is an irrational faculty, because it is not joined, as it is in man, with reason.

It is reason which distinguishes man from the brute. Its function is to discriminate between good and evil, justice and injustice, its operations being made manifest in the wonderful achievements of art, science, and letters. Whereas memory locks away the images of things both concrete and abstract, it is reason that releases them and gives them outward expression. And since God is the fount of all being and all knowledge, reason alone can enable man to approach God and gaze upon infinite and undefiled wisdom. Rightly employed it leads to perfection, but, wrongfully abused, casts down into evil. Reason, therefore, lies at the root of all sin.

The will, whose function it is to consent, unites with reason and is then called *liberum arbitrium*, free will, a natural faculty common to God, the devil, and the whole rational creation. Free will can never be lost, diminished, or coerced, for whatever it chooses, even if it chooses under external pressure, is chosen without internal constraint. No weakness of the senses, no defect of reason or memory can make a man evil. What makes him evil is the perverse employment of free will, the conscious rejection of the promptings of right reason. Salvation, therefore, and damnation depend upon the right or wrong use of free will. To will is a natural act. To will good, however, is beyond the powers of unaided nature. Are there, then, two wills in man, one reaching out to

good, the other inclining to evil? Or is there only one will
which, no matter how disturbed by unruly passion, the
beguilements of the devil and the enticements of man,
always retains its integrity? The answer is that the will remains integral. But it needs grace in order to choose the
good, for, of the possible alternatives, the ability to sin, the
ability not to sin, the inability not to sin and the inability to
sin, only the last belongs to God: the first and second
belonged to Adam in paradise, whilst the third, the inability
not to sin, belongs to man in his present state.

Sin brought death into the world, and sin, in a manner of
speaking, inflicts death on the soul. Can the soul, then, really
die? Plants, animals, and men die because in them body and
soul can be separated. Even the souls of animals can die,
because being composed of airy substance they are subject to
disintegration. But the human soul is a simple, incomposite
nature. It cannot be disintegrated. It is life, and life cannot
die any more than fire can grow cold. Furthermore, the soul
grasps and retains abstract mathematical principles which are
unchangeable and, on the supposition that only like can unite
with like, the soul must also be unchangeable. Finally, it can
attain wisdom, and wisdom is immortal.

Book III opens with a discussion of the gospel text which
says that Lazarus' soul was received into heavens by angels.
To understand the precise meaning of this, it should be
recalled that there are in man four powers: one which perceives colours, sounds, tastes; one which compares images
impressed on the senses and recreates by the imagination
other images from them; one which discerns truth from falsehood; and one, the intellectual power, which transcends all
earthly images and attains the source of all truth.

The power of imagination keeps man tethered to earth not
only during his waking hours but also during sleep. God
makes use of this power to instruct the good and to punish
the wicked. When the soul is tormented in dreams, does it

actually suffer? The answer is that stones, which are bereft of sense, cannot feel pain, but that man, even when he is asleep, can be aware of it. Therefore, if in sleep he sees images of people and hears them speaking, and thereby experiences fear or suffering, the words he hears are imaginary, but the truth they convey is real. Applying this conclusion to the state of the soul when it has been separated from the body, the meaning of the Lazarus parable becomes clear.

As long as the soul resides in the body, it employs bodily organs and receives corporeal images. But during sleep it sees itself in imaginary situations, sometimes experiencing pleasure, at other times torment. In the same way, when the soul is released from its earthly bonds, it sees itself in an imaginary body in which it is welcomed by angels to be consoled or tormented. In the Lazarus story Dives saw himself with an imaginary body in a certain situation, in which he was subjected to punishment. Were the fires with which he was burned imaginary? Most commentators on this story have admitted them to be real. But since material fires burn corporeal elements, it is doubtful whether they could torture a spiritual being like the soul. Saint Gregory solved the question by saying that the soul suffers not by feeling the fire, but by seeing it, little realising that if the soul has corporeal vision, it should also have corporeal feeling. Saint Augustine, on the other hand, was of the opinion that the devils possess bodies which would be sensitive to material fire. But even if this view is unacceptable, there seems no illogicality in admitting that as the soul is contained in a human body, so it may be contained and burned in a corporeal fire.

Not all souls suffer torment after death, but of those who do, it is merely a means of purifying them before they attain eternal bliss. Those who accuse God of cruelty because he creates those who are destined to eternal torment, fail to recognize his mercy in allowing such creatures to run their allotted span on earth instead of consigning them immediately

to hell. But some are born to wrath, others for glory. To the
latter everything conspires to their good, whilst to the others
everything conspires to evil. If purgatorial punishments are
such, what are the consolations? Are they, like the punishments, corporeal? The reply is that, since God already gives
spiritual consolation to those who live well on earth, he will
bestow the same kind of reward after death. It will take the
form of infused knowledge, understanding of mysteries and
converse with angels. The upright soul, in contrast to the sinful soul, does not pass through the torment of fire, but finds
rest immediately in the bosom of God. In order to learn what
happens on earth it has no need to move from place to place,
because it dwells in him who fills heaven and earth. Because
some souls are more perfect than others they are allocated to
different 'mansions' according to their dignity and degree;
but each one enjoys his own particular bliss. If, on the one
hand, those who are not perfect need our prayers to assist
them in attaining beatitude, the perfect, on the other, help
us. They are conscious of our needs, see all our desires, and
present our prayers to God. 'Let us, then, with what devotion we can command, honour the saints, praise them, glorify
them, contemplate their bliss, imitate their good deeds, and
aspire to join their company. All their care is for us, and they
pray the more earnestly for us as they realise that their
happiness cannot be consummated without us.'

THE SOURCES

In order to place Aelred's ideas in their context it may be
useful to examine one or two fundamental questions that
puzzled the best minds of the twelfth century. Some of these
problems were not finally elucidated until the time of the
great scholastics, but the endeavours of earlier investigators
throw into relief the teachings which eventually gained acceptance. Whilst most writers were agreed on the general outline

of medieval psychology, there were several points on which Augustine, from whom they derived their ideas, had not expressed a firm conviction. On such topics individual interpretation differed widely. The points that appear to have allowed the widest scope for speculation on the nature of the soul were concerned with its definition, its origin, its unity, and its substantiality.

By the middle of the twelfth century, when Aelred's *Dialogue* was composed, the choice of definition lay between the one proposed by Plato, in which the soul was considered as the principle of self-movement, and the one proposed by Aristotle, in which the soul was the form of the body.[21] The platonic conception was accepted by Augustine and his followers, Cassiodorus,[22] Isidore,[23] Rhabanus Maurus[24] and Alcuin.[25] But, wishing to guard against the excessive spiritualism which saw the whole man only in the soul, the body being a mere prison or instrument, Augustine clarified his ideas in successive definitions until he reached a formula which described man as neither angel nor beast, but a nature composed of both.[26] This teaching held the field practically unchanged in subsequent centuries. William of Conches,[27] however, was led by his study of Chalcidius' commentary on Plato's *Timaeus* to push the idea of the soul as a principle of self-movement to its extreme conclusion. He felt that the life and movement in plants, animals, and men came from a world soul, and that this force, which expressed itself in various ways according to the nature of the bodies it informed, was the Holy Ghost. This radical and novel theory aroused antagonism and was attacked by William of Saint Thierry in a letter addressed to Saint Bernard, in which he complained that Platonism was undermining the foundations of the christian faith.[28]

Aelred makes no allusion to this controversy and takes his stand on traditional teaching. For him the soul was 'a rational life, changeable in time though not in space, immortal in certain respects and capable of experiencing happiness or misery'.

It is evident from an analysis and elaboration of the terms of this definition that he was writing quite independently of his two cistercian contemporaries, William of Saint Thierry[29] and Alcher of Clairvaux,[30] the first of whom gives two definitions of the soul and the latter four. His formula is essentially augustinian and is uninfluenced by the newer currents of thought.

The extent of the difficulties presented to christian thinkers by the problem of the origin of the soul may be measured by the hesitations of Augustine and his followers. At the beginning of his enquiries Augustine had unquestioningly accepted platonic pre-existence theory, which considered the soul to have existed eternally like universal forms.[31] But the more he studied sacred scripture, the less tenable this view seemed.[32] Even less acceptable was the manichaean and gnostic position that the soul emanated from the divine substance: on this supposition the degrading changes of the soul would be attributable to God.[33] He also found Tertullian's traducianist theory, according to which the soul is propagated by the parents, unspeakably perverse.[34] In this uncertain state of mind he addressed a series of questions to Saint Jerome,[35] but on receiving Jerome's creationist solution that the soul was formed directly by God, he rejected it, perceiving that it provided no satisfactory explanation of original sin. In the end Augustine committed himself to no particular theory, but was inclined to favour a kind of spiritual Traducianism, according to which the soul is born from the souls of the parents. His hesitation was reflected in his followers throughout the whole of the Middle Ages.[36] With the passage of time the creationist theory gained more ground and by the twelfth century was the common belief.[37] There were, however, in spite of the almost unanimous opposition of the school of Laon,[38] a few remaining adherents of the Traducianist theory.[39]

Aelred's approach to this problem was complicated by the heretical theories of his day regarding the value of baptism.

The creationist opinion that the soul was formed immediately by God would lead to the conclusion that it was created sinless and in no need of the cleansing waters of baptism, and his expression of such a view might implicate him in the unorthodox tenets of the manichaean sects. On the other hand the traducianist theory had been almost universally abandoned. He therefore adopted a middle course, somewhat like Augustine's spiritual Traducianism, saying that the soul is produced from an invisible and intangible substance, as from a kind of matter, emanating from the parents' affections. This view was put forward tentatively, 'as an opinion rather than an affirmation'.

As to the moment when the soul is infused into the body Augustine furnished no specific answer. Origen had believed that the soul was created at the same time as the angels, and was later imprisoned in the body as a result of sin, whereas Gregory of Nyssa held that body and soul were created simultaneously.[40] Later on, when medical teaching had been assimilated by ecclesiastical writers, two theories prevailed: one, that the soul was infused into the body at the moment of conception; the other, that the soul was infused after forty days, when the lineaments of a human being had been formed. Both these views were mentioned by Cassiodorus.[41] Most twelfth-century writers were in agreement with the second view.[42] Though Aelred makes no specific mention of the forty days that should elapse between the conception of the body and the infusion of the soul, he was probably familiar with this teaching, for he says in his usual guarded manner that the soul unites with the body 'after a certain time when the body is provided with sense'.

The extreme dualism taught by the Platonists made union between body and soul difficult to reconcile. Augustine thought that it could be explained only on the assumption that God so willed it.[43] Instead, therefore, of there being a natural hostility between body and soul, there must exist a natural love.[44] But since love arises only between things that have similarities with one another, a ground for likeness must be discovered; otherwise the union between two such contrary natures, one spiritual, the other material, must remain a complete mystery. Three main solutions were suggested: union through number and harmony; the intervention of a physical medium; and the binding together in the unity of a person.

The first theory, based on the pythagorean and platonic doctrine of the harmonic relation of numbers, held that body and soul are knit together by the power of harmony.[45] The body must possess a definite organisation and its members must be in perfect relation and harmony; only in this way could the soul employ it as a suitable vehicle of its functions.[46] The soul has no love for the body as such: what it loves are the harmony and proportion existing between the various parts of the body. As long as this harmony continues, the soul remains united to the body, but if it is disturbed or lost, the soul withdraws.[47]

For those who could not accept the abstract similarity of harmony between soul and body, the principle that like unites with like was a compelling reason for seeking a likeness in the physical sphere. But because the gross materiality of the body ruled out any likeness with a spiritual soul, writers sought for a physical medium. Augustine had already envisaged such a medium, but theologians were loath to admit a third spirit in man, which would be different from both the soul and the Holy Spirit. William of Conches circumvented this difficulty by borrowing ideas from Constantinus Africanus and describing the medium as being identical with the airy substance from which the souls of animals are formed;[48] but he also conceived of a medium which, for its subtlety, could easily be termed spirit. Isaac of Stella, on the other hand, placed the medium in the two extremes of body and soul, the highest point of the body and the lowest point of the soul, *sensualitas carnis* and *phantasticum animae*.[49] This union of highest and lowest was, for Isaac, a law of cosmic order parallelled in the five degrees of knowledge which, like Jacob's ladder, reached from earth to heaven.[50] So, the highest function of the body, which is the imagination of corporeal things, is the connecting link with the lowest faculty of the rational soul, which is the imagination of spiritual things.

Aelred has a doctrine which bears some similarity to this, but he does not elaborate it to the same extent as Isaac. He says that the body, composed of the gross elements of earth and water, can be united to the body only through a medium which contains the subtle elements of fire and air. This medium is the *sensualis vis,* which combines qualities common to both body and spirit. It draws its constitutive elements from the body, but is so akin to spirit that it might almost be called a spirit.

The third solution for the union of body and soul is the binding together in the unity of a person. Hugh of Saint Victor advanced the view that there is a difference between the union that arises from the combination of two things which in coming together form a unity, and the union which ensues from the communication of unity by one thing to another.[51] Walls, roof, and foundations are three separate things, and none of them taken individually makes a house. When they are added together, all three things are compounded, not two things to a third. But in the case of body and soul, this is not so. The soul, in so far as it is a rational spirit, has personality, and when the body is joined to it, it is compounded not to form a person but to share in a person: *non tantum ad personam componitur quantum in personam apponitur.*[52] And so the soul, which is the principle of unity, confers unity on the body to which it is joined.

From the terms used by Aelred we are led to infer that he believes body and soul to be commingled, but he adds the saving phrase that, just as the two natures of Christ are united through the medium of the soul to form one person, so the two substantial principles of the human person are united through the medium of sense.

Through his interest in the unity and simplicity of the soul and in the identity of the ego with its acts, Augustine was led to conclude that all the powers of the soul were substantially identical with the soul and with each other. Since he was the supreme authority on this question all subsequent writers,[53] with the sole exception of Claudianus Mamertus,[54] echoed his teaching.

The main problem that confronted writers of the twelfth century was that of reconciling the manifold acts of sensible apprehension with the uniqueness of the soul's substance. Isaac of Stella put forward the supposition that there was a particular organ of the soul by which its activities could be differentiated. But this was only a partial solution. It was felt that underlying the various acts of feeling, imagining, reasoning, and understanding there must be various powers at work and that these powers must be distinct from the soul. Isaac had said that the 'properties' and the virtues of the soul were not identical with it. But these powers were not substances; they could not be contrasted with the soul as substance against substance. They were distinct from it as is a disposition from a substance. They were, in fact, modifications of the soul's substance. Thus, the powers of the soul were 'unfoldings' of the soul just as the acts were unfoldings of the powers. This explanation, which owes something to the aristotelian concepts of subject and accident, was put forward by Hugh of Saint Victor,[56] and was followed by others, such as John of Salisbury,[57] Robert of Melun[58] and Richard of Saint Victor.[59]

Aelred's explanation is simpler and more traditional. For him the soul is an incorporeal substance having three faculties which cannot be separated either in operation or thought. Though the faculties are in the soul, they do not exist there as accidents, but are one and the same substance as the soul itself. Just as the three Persons of the Trinity are one God, so reason, memory, and will are three words denoting one substance.

This brief outline of Aelred's teaching on the main problem connected with the soul shows that he kept strictly to the ideas put forward by Saint Augustine. He made no claim to originality and contented himself with providing a synthesis of the ideas culled from the voluminous works of him whom he called 'that inimitable man, who left nothing untouched'. His approach to this subject shows great differences as regards thought, method, and sources from that adopted by his three religious colleagues and contemporaries, William of Saint Thierry, Isaac of Stella, and Alcher of Clairvaux. William, in his *De natura corporis et animae,* written in his declining years, combines ideas taken from Augustine, Gregory of Nyssa,[60] Scotus Eriugena,[61] Ambrose[62] and Plotinus,[63] and thereby displays more learning and a wider range of sources. Though he agrees with Aelred on most points of augustinian psychology, he differs from him considerably on medical and anatomical theories, which he had derived from Greek and Arabic authors through the medium of Constantinus Africanus. As a well-trained and acute theologian he compares favourably with Aelred, but he does not express his psychological ideas with the same clarity and searching analysis as is found in the *Dialogue.* Aelred's work has greater breadth, its inspiration is more uniform, its method is more logical, and its humanism and charm are more pervasive.

The *De anima* of Isaac of Stella was written to Alcher of Clairvaux in response to a request for an analysis of the essence of the soul.[64] Its aim, therefore, is limited. It does not pretend to deal with all the questions covered by Aelred's *Dialogue.* Isaac, however, gives proof of metaphysical understanding of real depth. His answers hint at great reserves of knowledge sparingly used, and in them we see glimpses of that bold philosophical and theological speculation which later on, to the chagrin of his monks, was deliberately restrained. In the employment of his sources he is more

varied than Aelred, whilst on medical matters he appears to be
as well informed as William of Saint Thierry. In short, his
work shows the profound penetration of spirituality by meta-
physics at that period and attests to a diffusion in the middle
of the twelfth century of a kind of abstract Platonism.

The treatise *De spiritu et anima*[65] is a work of a totally different calibre. Of its author we know nothing. None of the
catalogues of the great cistercian libraries of Cîteaux, Clairvaux, Pontigny and Fontenay mention the writer by name,
and the work, wherever it appears in medieval catalogues, is
always placed under the name of Augustine. To this attribu-
tion it owes its immense popularity and authority. It is the
Histoire Littéraire which has ascribed it to Alcher of
Clairvaux.[66]

The treatise, which has thirty-three chapters in the works
of Hugh of Saint Victor,[67] forty-four in the *Bibliotheca
Patrum Cisterciensium,*[68] and sixty-six in the works of Saint
Augustine,[69] has considerable didactic value. It is, however,
loosely knit together, has no logical sequence, is repetitive
and sometimes contradictory, and betrays here and there a
superficial understanding of the texts it contains. It enjoyed
almost universal authority for the greater part of a century
and its prestige among the scholastics was considerable. This
may be measured by the attitude of Albert the Great and
Thomas Aquinas, the latter of whom, only after prolonged
hesitation, was constrained to express his disbelief in Saint
Augustine's authorship.[70] In comparison with Aelred's
Dialogue it suffers primarily as a synthesis. In its breadth of
scholarship it is admittedly superior, but this is offset by the
lack of coordination in its parts. It is completely impersonal,
a stolid compilation put together without art or sensitivity,
bereft of any comment, explanation or suggestion. To this,
perhaps, it owes its success as a school manual, for it provides
a variety of texts in easily-accessible form.

As one reads the *Dialogue* it becomes apparent that Aelred's ideas had changed comparatively little with the passage

of the years. The thoughts expressed in previous works re-appear in a new setting, more fully developed, perhaps, and more clearly expounded. But his fundamental outlook remained the same. This shows that, towards the latter part of his life, he had to a large extent dispensed with personal investigation. This is not surprising in view of his sickness and his heavy administrative duties. But it detracts in no way from his achievement nor from the value and significance of the *Dialogue*. Rather does it enable us to measure the extent of his reading and his grasp of ideas and to form a judgement of Walter Daniel's testimony on his intellectual attainments.

Despite the insistence of cistercian tradition that the true occupation of the monk was the recital of the liturgical hours and manual labor,[71] Aelred, with the encouragement of Saint Bernard, pursued his interest in the cultivation of letters. His reading of the *De amicitis* of Cicero at the school in Hexham as a boy had fostered in him the sympathies of a true humanist, and these sympathies were never laid aside.[72] Though he had spent the greater part of his youth 'amidst the pots and pans'[73] of the scottish court and thereby lost the opportunity of being trained, as were many of his contemporaries, in the schools beyond the seas, the instinct to turn to the great minds of the past for counsel and guidance never left him. But he remained acutely aware of his lack of education and, even in his old age, when his eminence as a writer and a scholar was assured, he described himself in a sermon as 'a simple unlettered man, more like a fisherman than an orator'.[74] This personal appraisement of his attainments is far too modest. From those who knew him intimately we learn that, though his school-learning was slight, he became, through assiduous reading and the disciplined exercise of his acute natural powers, more cultured than many who were the products of the schools.[75] The puzzled admiration of Walter Daniel, his biographer, at the fusion in Aelred's personality of religious idealism, administrative efficiency, and literary ability is a veiled admission of the limitations of the mere scholastic mind.[76]

Aelred's theological and philosophical knowledge can have been acquired only in the cloister from a study of the Scriptures and the Fathers. He would learn much, too, from his seniors at Rievaulx, who reflected and perhaps handed down the theological opinions and culture of Saint Bernard, for it must be remembered that the founders of Rievaulx came from France. By consulting them, by discussing with his associates and disciples, who had been trained in the schools, the current problems in church matters, he acquired a firm and solid understanding of theological problems. His closest friendships were with men of the highest intellectual standing and he appears to have been able to speak with them on terms of equality. His first contact with Saint Bernard took place in 1142, shortly after Bernard's clash with Abelard at Sens, and it may be presumed that Aelred would learn much about that controversy which would sharpen his interest and deepen his understanding. Whether he accompanied his friend, Henry Murdach, archbishop of York, to the Council of Rheims where certain doctrines of Gilbert de la Porrée were being attacked, is not known.[77] What is certain is that for the greater part of his twenty years in office at Rievaulx he was a constant visitor to France and must have been aware of the controversies in which Saint Bernard was involved. The possibility that he may have met on these occasions John of Salisbury,[78] Robert Pullus[79] and Robert of Melun[80] cannot be ruled out, for we may infer from his remarks about current heresies,[81] the christological controversy in which Abelard and Peter Lombard were involved[82] and his veiled references to problems concerning Church and State[83] that he was no mere idle spectator of these affairs.

Apart from these tenuous possibilities there are definite traces in his writings of doctrines that link him with the school of Laon. The chief characteristic of this school was its

avoidance of speculation and its preoccupation with the
question of Creation, the origin of the soul, and the trans-
mission of original sin.[84] Hand in hand with this went an
avoidance of dialectic, a blind reliance on the Fathers, and a
loyal adherence to the teachings of Saint Augustine.[85] All
these characteristics are prominent in the writings of Aelred.
This does not imply that Aelred had studied the *Sentences*
of Laon or that he was directly dependent on them. But it is
not beyond the bounds of possibility that he had some
acquaintance with them. There was a strong following of the
Laon school in England, and at Durham, where Aelred was a
frequent visitor, a collection of the *Sentences* was in the
library. On all the main problems discussed in the *De anima*,
Aelred and the compilers of the *Sentences* agree: the questions asked, the answers given, and the order in which they
are treated are the same. This adherence to a particular
school of thought goes far to explain Aelred's apparent timi-
dity in dealing with certain problems. His almost servile
reliance on Augustine, his diffidence in expounding his personal opinions, and his failure to express his usual independent views, these and certain other anomalies can be
explained only on the assumption that he was bound to a
particular theological tradition. Where answers were already
settled and defined there was no room for speculation.

On the other hand, we see in the *Dialogue* that he put no
restrictions on those who questioned him. His disciples were
at liberty to doubt, to contradict, and to hold diametrically
opposed views to those he himself held. He was no doctri-
naire. He sympathised with the efforts of bold speculative
thinkers to find solutions to old questions. His antagonism
was reserved for the 'ignorant and fanatical', who, in face of
almost universal condemnation persisted in their perverse
doctrines and unseemly practices. It was pride and arrogance
of mind rather than the expression of erroneous doctrines
that Aelred found difficult to condone. To fall into error was
human, but to persist in disseminating doctrines that had

been proved to be false was, in his judgement, the height of folly and presumption.

Little else remains to be said. All Aelred's works were written in Latin in accordance with the custom of his times. But English was never far from his mind, and when he lay on his death bed it was in English that he uttered his final words because, as Walter Daniel said, English is easier on the tongue and sweeter to the ear. Perhaps for that reason he will look with a sympathetic eye on this attempt to put into his mother tongue the ideas he so elegantly expressed in Latin.

NOTES TO INTRODUCTION

1. J. Raine, The *Priory of Hexham* (Surtees Society, 1864) I: p. li / F. M. Powicke, *Walter Daniel's Life of Ailred, abbot of Rievaulx* (London, 1950) pp. xxxiv-vi (hereafter cited as *Vita*) A. Squire, *Aelred of Rievaulx. A Study* (London, 1969).

2. Aelred, *De genealogia Regum Anglorum;* PL 195:736-7.

3. *Vita Ailredi*, ed. Powicke, p. 3.

4. *Ibid.* p. 5

5. *Speculum charitatis;* PL 195:562.

6. M. D. Knowles, 'The Case of Saint William of York', *Cambridge Historical Journal*, V, 2 (1936) 162-77. It was during this journey that Aelred met Saint Bernard and was persuaded to write the *Speculum charitatis:* A. Wilmart, 'L'Instigateur du Speculum Charitatis d'Aelrède, abbé de Rievaulx,' *Revue d'Ascétique et de Mystique* (1933) 389-90.

7. Revesby was founded 9 August 1142. F. M. Powicke is incorrect in stating (*Vita*, p. lxii) that Aelred was chosen by abbot William of Rievaulx to be the superior. Aelred was elected by those who were to be sent (*mittendi fuerant*) to make the foundation: *Vita* p. 27.

8. Horstmann, *Nova Legenda Anglie*, II, 549.

9. *Vita*, p. 37.

10. *Speculum charitatis;* PL 195:563.

11. *Vita*, p. 38.

12. J. Turk, 'Charta Caritatis Prior', (*Analecta Sacri Ordinis Cisterciensis*, 1 (1945) p. 59 / J.-B. Mahn, *L'Ordre cistercien et son gouvernement* (Paris, 1945) 217 ff.

13. *Vita*, pp. 25, 42.

14. *Vita*, 49: 'quasi membrane folium' is Walter Daniel's description.

15. *Vita*, 40.

16. *Vita*, 61.

17. J. T. Muckle, 'The Doctrine of St. Gregory of Nyssa on Man as the Image of God,' *Mediaeval Studies*, 7 (1945) 55-84 / M. Standaert, 'La doctrine de l'image chez S. Bernard, *Ephemerides Theologicae Lovanienses*, 23 (1947) 70-129.

18. PG 44:127-239. P. Courcelle, ' "Connais-toi toi-même" de Socrate à S. Bernard', *Études augustiniennes* (1974-75,) 3 vols. / A. Maiorino Tuozzi, *La 'conoscenza de sé' nella scuola cisterciense*

(Naples: *Istituto italiano per gli studi storici*, 1976).

19.   E. Gilson, 'Regio dissimilitudinis de Platon à Saint Bernard de Clairvaux', *Mediaeval Studies,* 9 (1947) 108 ff: J. C. Didier, 'Pour la fiche "regio dissimilitudinis",' *Melanges de Sciences religieuses,* 8 (1951) 205-210: P. Courcelle, 'Tradition néoplatonicienne et traditions chrétiennes de la 'region de dissemblance' (Platon Politique 273d)', *Archives d'Histoire doctrinale et littéraire du Moyen Âge,* 24 (1957) 24 (1957) 5-33. See also R. Tremblay, 'La théorie psychologique de la Trinité chez Saint Augustin, *Cahiers de théologie et de philosophie* (Ottawa, 1952).

20.   *Speculum charitatis;* PL 195:502-619.

21.   *Platonis Timaeus interprete Chalcidio,* ed. J. Wrobel (Leipzig, 1876) c. ccxxi, p. 236 / Aristotle, *De anima,* II, 1.

22.   *De anima;* PL 70:1283a.

23.   *De differentiis,* II, 27; PL 83:83bc.

24.   *Tractatus de anima,* c. 1; PL 110:1110c.

25.   *De animae ratione,* c. x; PL 101:643d.

26.   Augustine's progress of mind may be traced through *De quantitate animae,* XIII,22; PL 32:1048. *De moribus ecclesiae catholicae,* I, xxvii,52; PL 32:1332, and *De Trinitate,* XV, vii, 11; PL 42:1065.

27.   *Comment. in Boethium,* in C. Jourdain, *Des Commentaires inédits de Guillaume de Conches* (Paris, 1862) p. 76 / H. Flatten, *Die Philosophie des Wilhelm von Conches* (Koblenz, 1929) pp. 151, 65 / Abelard, *Theologia Christiana;* PL 178:1145 / T. Gregory, *Anima Mundi: La filosofia di Guglielmo di Conches e la scuola di Chartres,* Publicazioni dell'Istituto di filosofia dell' Università di Roma, 3 (Florence, 1955) / T. Gregory, 'L'anima mundi' nella filosofia del XII secolo', *Giornale critico della Filosofia italiana,* 30 (1951) 494-508 / M. T. Gibson, 'The study of the "Timaeus" in the XIth and XIIth centuries, *Pensamiento,* 25 (1969) 183-194 / T. Gregory, *Platonismo medievale. Studi e ricerche. Istituto storico italiano per il medio evo, Studi storici* 26-27 (Rome, 1958).

28.   *De erroribus Guilelmi de Conchis;* PL 180:340.

29.   *De natura corporis et animae;* PL 180:707.

30.   *De spiritu et anima;* PL 40:781, 784, 788, 796, taken from Ambrose, Augustine, Alcuin and perhaps Hugh of Saint Victor.

31.   *De libero arbitrio,* III,20; PL 32:1298.

32.   *De civitate Dei,* XI,23; PL 41:336.

33.   *De genesi ad litteram,* VII, iii-iv, 4-6; PL 34:357-8; *Ep. ad Honoratum,* CXL, 7; PL 33:541.

34.   Ep. 190, 14; PL 33, 861.

35.   *Ep.* 166, c. iii; PL 33:723.

36. Cassiodorus, *De anima,* 2; PL 70:1292bc / Gregory, *Lib.* IX, *Ep.* 52; PL 77:990 / Isidore, *De differentiis,* II,30; PL 83:85d / Rhabanus Marus, *Tract. de anima,* c. ii; PL 110:1112cd.

37. Hugh of Saint Victor, *De sacramentis,* I,vii,29; PL 176:29 / Adelard of Bath, *De eodem et diverso,* ed. H. Willner (Münster, 1903) p. 79 / William of Conches, *Philosophia mundi;* PL 172:98c / William of Champeaux, *De origine animae,* c.ii, iii; PL 163:1043-4 / Abelard, *Hexaemeron;* PL 178:770a / Richard of Saint Victor, *De Trinitate,* IV, 16; PL 196:940a.

38. D. Lottin, 'Les théories sur le peché original au XIIe siècle', *Recherches de Théologie ancienne et médiévale,* 11 (Louvain, 1933) 17-33.

39. Odo of Cambrai, *De peccato originali,* 3; PL 160:1098-9.

40. *De opificio hominis;* PG 44:229.

41. *De anima,* c. vii; PL 70:1292b. *Cfr.* Rhabanus Maurus, *Tract. de anima,* ii; PL 110:1112bc.

42. William of Conches, *Philos.* IV,15; PL 172:90 / Odo of Cambrai, *De peccato originali,* III; PL 160:1097-8 / Robertus Pullus, *Sententiae,* II,7; PL 186:728b / Hugh of Saint Victor, *De sacramentis,* I, vii,30; PL 176:300c.

43. *Cfr.* Ambrose, *Ep.* I, 34; PL 16:1075a / Hugh of Saint Victor, *De sacramentis,* I,vi,1; PL 176:263c / William of Champeaux, *De origine animae,* c. iii; PL 163:1043-1044a / William of Saint Thierry, *De natura corporis et animae,* II; PL 180:712a.

44. *De genesi ad litteram,* VII; xxvii, 38; PL 34:369 / Cassiodorus, *De anima,* ii; PL 70:1283a / Rhabanus Maurus, *Tract. de anima,* 1; PL 110; 1111a / Honorius Augustodunensis, *Elucidarium,* II, 14; PL 172: 1145a / Richard of Saint Victor, *De Trinitate;* PL 196:947b.

45. Boethius, *De musica,* I,i; PL 63:1168d. *Cfr.* Gilbert de la Porrée, *Com. in lib. Boethii Quomodo substantiae bonae sint;* PL 64: 1322 / Boethius, *De musica,* I,i; PL 63:1169a: 'Id nimirum scientes quod tota nostrae animae corporisque compago musica coaptatione conjuncta sit'.

46. Claudianus Mamertus, *De statu animae,* I,6; PL 53:771 / Rhabanus Maurus, *De universo,* VI,1; PL 111:142 / Adelard of Bath, *Quaestiones naturales,* xliii & *De eodem et diverso,* ed. Willner, p. 23 / William of Saint Thierry, *De natura corporis et animae,* I, II; PL 180: 696, 712 / Isaac of Étoile, *De anima;* PL 194:1882cd.

47. Cassiodorus, *De anima,* ii; PL 70:1284c / Alcuin, *De animae ratione,* x; PL 101:644a.

48. *Dragmaticon,* p. 268.

49. *De anima;* PL 194:1881c. *Cfr.* Hugh of Saint Victor, *De unione*

corporis et spiritus; PL 177:285.

50.   K. Werner, Der *Entwicklungsgang der mittelalterlichen Psychologie* (Vienna, 1876).

51.   *De sacramentis,* II,i,11; PL 176:405-6.

52.   *De sacramentis,* II, i, 11; PL 176:408-9. This doctrine, from Odo of Cambrai (*De peccato originali,* III; PL 160:1087) was followed by other writers: *cfr.* Robert Pullus, *Sententiae* II,10, III,17-20 (PL 186:734, 784 ff.), Richard of Saint Victor, *De Trinitate,* IV,25 (PL 196:947-8), Robert of Melun, *Quaestiones de epistolis Pauli,* ed. Martin, p. 11-12.

53.   Gregorius, *Hom. in Ezech.* II,5; PL 76:990 / Isidore, *Etymologiae,* XI,1; PL 82:339 / Alcuin, *De animae ratione,* vi; PL 101: 641-2 / Rhabanus Maurus, *De universo,* VI,1; PL 111:141 / William of Saint Thierry, *De natura corporis et animae;* PL 180, 720.

54.   *De statu animae,* I, xxiv, xxvi; PL 53:729, 734-5.

55.   *De anima;* PL 194:1876-78, 1879d-1880a / Alcher of Clairvaux, *De spiritu et anima,* iv, 13; PL 40:782, 788.

56.   *De sacramentis,* I, iii, 21, 27; PL 176:225-228.

57.   *Metalogicon,* IV,9; PL 199:922.

58.   *Quaestiones de divina pagina,* q. 63, ed. Martin, p. 33.

59.   *Beniamin Minor,* xvii; PL 196:12.

60.   *De hominis opificio;* PG 44:127-239.

61.   *De divisione naturae,* IV, 11; PL 122:793.

62.   *Hexaemeron,* VI, vii-ix; PL 14:257-72.

63.   J. M. Déchanet, 'Guillaume et Plotin,' *Revue du Moyen Age latin, 2* (Strasbourg, 1946) 240-246. William also shows traces of Origen's *De principiis,* II, viii.

64.   F. Bliemetzrieder, 'Isaac von Stella. Beiträge zur Lebensbeschreibung', *Jahrbuch der Philosophie und spekulativen Theologie,* 15 (1904) 31; A. Fracheboud, 'Le Pseudo-Denys l'Aréopagite parmi les sources du cistercien Isaac de l'Étoile,' *Collectanea Ordinis Cisterciensium* (Westmalle, 1947-8) 328-341, 19-34. For an evaluation of his doctrine see also Bliemetzrieder, 'Isaac de Stella, sa speculation théologique', *Recherches de Théologie ancienne et médiévale,* 4 (1932) 132-158; E. Bertola, 'La dottrina psicologica di Isaaco di Stella', *Rivista filosofia neo-scolastica,* 45 (1953) 297-309.

65.   PL 40:779.

66.   *Histoire Littéraire,* XIII:683-6. Coustant, in his *Admonitio in libro de Spiritu et anima* does not definitely assign the authorship to Alcher.

67.   PL 177:165.

68.   Tom. VI, ed. Tissier, 84-103.

69. PL 40:779-832.
70. G. Théry, 'L'authenticité du "De Spiritu et Anima" dans Saint Thomas et Albert le Grand', *Revue des sciences philosophiques et théologiques, 10* (1921) 373-377.
71. Ph. Guignard, *Les monuments primitifs de la Règle Cistercienne* (Dijon, 1878) 79-250; *ibid. Statuta,* c. lviii, p. 266; D'Arbois de Jubainville, *L'État intérieur des abbayes Cisterciennes et en particular de Clairvaux au XIIe siècle.*
72. M. D. Knowles, 'The Humanism of the Twelfth Century', *Studies,* 28 (Dublin, 1941), 43-59.
73. *Speculum charitatis;* PL 195:502-3.
74. *Sermones Inediti,* ed. C. H. Talbot (Rome, 1952).
75. *Vita S. Waltheni;* Acta Sanctorum, August, I:258.
76. *Vita Ailredi,* p. 26.
77. John of Salisbury, *Historia Pontificalis,* ed. Poole, p. 18; N. M. Häring, 'A Latin Dialogue on the Doctrine of Gilbert of Poitiers,' *Mediaeval Studies,* 15 (1953) 243-289; *id.* 'The Cistercian Everard of Ypres and his Appraisal of the Conflict between St. Bernard and Gilbert of Poitiers, *Mediaeval Studies,* 19 (1957) 143-172; *id.* 'The Writings against Gilbert of Poitiers by Geoffrey of Auxerre,' *Analecta Cisterciensia,* 22 (1966), 2-83.
78. A passage in the *Policraticus,* I, v, (ed. Webb) I, 42d has been based upon a passage from Aelred. No one seems to have adverted to John's many borrowings from Saint Bernard.
79. A. Pelster, 'Einige Angaben über Leben und Schriften des Robertus Pullus,' *Scholastik,* 12 (1937) 234-47; F. Courtney, 'Cardinal Robert Pullen. An English Theologian of the Twelfth Century', *Analecta Gregoriana,* 64 (Rome, 1954); A. Landgraf, 'Studien zur Theologie des XII Jahrhunderts: Robert Pullus und P. Lombard und P. Abelard', *Traditio,* 1:214-220. His sermons are often found together with those of Aelred and there was a collection of them at Rievaulx, M. R. James, *Catalogue of Manuscripts in Jesus College, Cambridge,* p. 48.
80. The *Sententiae* of Robert of Melun seem to have found sympathetic readers in cistercian houses judging by the provenance of existing manuscripts: R. M. Martin, *Oeuvres de Robert de Melun,* I, xv-xvii.
81. *De anima,* end of book I.
82. The *Eulogium magistri Joannis de Cornubia* was in the Rievaulx library and the exact words discussed by John, namely *tunica* and *tunicatum,* are used by Aelred in one of his sermons among the *Sermones inediti.*

83.   *De oneribus, sermo* XI; PL 195:403.

84.   John of Salisbury, *Historia Pontificalis*, viii, (ed. Poole) p. 20. The manuscript of the *Liber Pancrisis*, Ms. Troyes 425, came from Clairvaux (edited by G. Lefèbre, *Anselmi Laudunensis et Radulfi fratris eius sententias excerptas,* [Paris, 1895]). Saint Bernard, who took part in the controversies in which the two brothers were involved, was friendly towards them, *Ep.* 13; PL 182:116-7. It is worth noting that the *Sententiae Divinae Paginae,* ed. Bliemetzrieder, from the cistercian abbey of Heiligenkreuz, were bound together with the *Capitula Remis... collecta contra Magistrum Gilbertum,* which were derived from the work of Geoffrey of Clairvaux's *Contra capitula Gilberti Pictaviensis episcopi* (PL 185:595-617). The sentences of Anselm and his brother were quoted by the cistercian in Idung's *Dialogue between a Cluniac and a Cistercian; Cistercians and Cluniacs: The Case for Cîteaux,* CF 33: p. 54.

85.   R. Silvain, 'La tradition des sentences d'Anselme de Laon', *Archives d'histoire doctrinale et littéraire du Moyen Age,* 15 (1947-8) 14; V. J. Flint, 'The "School of Laon": A Reconsideration.' *Recherches de théologie ancienne et médiévale,* 43 (1976) 89-110. Further discoveries of links between the School of Laon and Cîteaux are mentioned by I. P. Sheldon-Williams, 'Eriugena and Cîteaux,' *Studia Monastica,* 19 (1977) 76-92.

AELRED OF RIEVAULX

DIALOGUE ON THE SOUL

HERE BEGINS THE DIALOGUE
OF AELRED, THE VENERABLE ABBOT
OF RIEVAULX, CONCERNING
THE SOUL

AELRED. What is the reason, John, for this unexpected visit of yours?

JOHN. I have read something in the works of Saint Augustine which has somewhat disturbed me, and I should like to have your help and ask your opinion about certain questions.

AELRED. I am at your service. For now that these people have finished the business for which they came, they have departed.

JOHN. I should like to know what you think about the soul. For Augustine does not have the same ideas about it as I have been accustomed to hold. He says that it does not move in space and consequently is not contained in a place, that it is not circumscribed by local boundaries, and that it has neither length, breadth, nor height.*

*Aug. Gen. 8,22,43 (389); 7,21,27 (365); Trin. 10,7,9 (978); Cassiod. An. 2 (1283C); Rhaban.An.1 (111A); Mamert, Stat.1,16 (718C).

AELRED. Well, what about it? Do you think otherwise?

JOHN. Completely. Do I not feel that my soul is contained in my body? And since my body is a place, I cannot see how the soul can fail to be in a place and be moved from place to place with the body.

AELRED. There has been no lack of very learned men who felt that the soul was in no way contained in the body, but rather that

*Aug.Quant.30,
61 (1069).

*Aug.Gen.7,3,4
(357).

the soul contained the body;* and standing
firmly in its own nature it imparts existence
to the body subjected to it,* not taking
existence from it. When the soul ceases to
vivify the body, do all the members   not fall
asunder? Does not the flesh putrefy, the
bones dry up and the whole unity of the parts
break up?

JOHN. Does anyone doubt that, as long as
I live, my soul is in my body?

AELRED. What of it? Although it can be
said with reason that the soul is in the body, is
it therefore necessary that it should be in the
body as in a place and be moved with
the body?

JOHN. So I understand.

AELRED. According to the christian faith
the soul is made to the likeness of God.

JOHN. Nothing is more certain.

AELRED. And God's word is: 'I fill heaven
and earth'.* Hence the pagan, who thought
that Jupiter was God, said after deeply
pondering the divine nature, 'All things are
full of Jove'.* Since, therefore, God fills
all things, does he fill them as water fills a
vase or air a bladder?

JOHN. Not at all.

AELRED. How then?

JOHN. When I was a boy and argued with
other boys and the question arose how God
could be everywhere, the answer we were
told to give was that God is everywhere not
locally, but by the exercise of his power.

AELRED. I say that God is everywhere not only by his power, but also by his
essence.* For his power is not one thing and

*Jer 23:24. Cf.
Sent.Band.1,37,
42(1015B).

*Vergil, Eclog.3,
60(7); Cassiod.
An 2(1283); Aug.
Gen 7,21,42
(389); Sent.
Berol.(55).

*Aug.SMM 2,5,18
(1277); Sent.Ans.
(151); Sent.Div.
pag. (212, no.
292); Hugo, Dial.
6,6(1222A);Sent.
Pull.1,9(689). Cf.
Abel.Theol.sch.
3,6(1106).

his essence another. So that he who is believed, and with truth, is to be nowhere according to place, is believed to be everywhere by his essence. For to him essence and omnipotent power are the same.* So the human soul, made in the image of its creator, acts in its own body in somewhat the same fashion as does God in all his creatures.* Therefore it fills its whole body, but not locally. For if it were diffused or extended locally, it would also be greater in the whole than in the part. And so it is everywhere in the body that is subject to it, if not filling it, nonetheless imitating the likeness of him who is everywhere in all his creatures.*

JOHN. It would be wrong for me to doubt that, as regards God, this is so. But I am unable to understand how it is so either of God or of the soul.

AELRED. Well, accepting on the basis of faith that it is true of God, let us find out how it applies to the soul, which is made to the likeness of God. For perhaps, when you have found the image, you will more easily find him of whom it is the image.

JOHN. Very well.

AELRED. Have you any doubt that the soul is in the body?

JOHN. Clearly I have no doubt. But I cannot see how it can be in the body without being in a place.

AELRED. Is it in your whole body or only in part of it?

JOHN. Of course it is in the whole and in all its parts with the exception of the hair and nails and any other parts that lack feeling.*

*Aug.Joan,20,4 (1553); Cassiod. An.2(1287).

*Aug.Gen.7,3,4 (357); Mamert, Stat.3,2(761); Alcuin, An.rat.8 (643A); William, Nat.corp.(719D); Alcher, Spir, 35 (805); Sent.div. pag.(21).

*Aug.Ep.166,2,4 (722); Cassiod. An.2(1284C).

*Aug.Gen.7,16, 23(363).

In these there is no indication of the presence of the soul.

AELRED. You are mistaken, brother. Do not the nails and the hair grow even after a man is dead?

JOHN. That is a good reminder.

AELRED. Therefore the soul is in even the smallest finger.*

Aug.Ep.Man.16, 20(185).

JOHN. I agree.

AELRED. Is it the whole soul or only a part of it?

JOHN. Do not laugh at me if I say some part of it, since I cannot understand anything else yet.

AELRED. Far be it from me to laugh, for we are trying to find out not what is to be believed, but what is to be understood. If therefore some part of the soul is in the finger, what happens to that part when the finger is cut off?

JOHN. Why should I not say of the soul what I say of the body, namely that both are diminished?

AELRED. So if the feet or hands of anyone are cut off, if the eyes are pulled out, if the ears are struck off, then it follows that the soul is diminished to the same extent as the body? And a mutilated man will have a smaller soul than a whole man.

JOHN. This is absurd and quite unacceptable to the human mind. For if someone has lost a member, he certainly feels that his body lacks something, but he does not feel that the nature of his soul is different from before, or that it is wounded, divided or in any way changed.*

Aug.Quant. 32,67(1072): Mamert,Stat. 1,17(719).

AELRED. Splendid and very clearly stated. You see how you are convinced by reason that the soul is not made up of parts, but that its essence is simple and not composite,* that it cannot be cut up, divided, locally extended, stretched out, or spread out.

Aug.Quant. 1,2(1036).

JOHN. I see that I have great difficulty in understanding this, because I now know that I was ignorant of my ignorance,* that I do not know what the soul is. The first thing, therefore, is for you to instruct me on that point, otherwise I shall appear to argue about something which is not the soul rather than about the soul itself.

Mamert, Stat. 3,11,2(773).

AELRED. I would be more willing to say what the soul is not, rather than boldly state what it is.

JOHN. If you are willing, I am prepared to hear this first.

AELRED. The soul is not a body nor the likeness of a body: it is not earth, air, fire or water, nor is it anything that is made up from these four, or from three of them, and certainly not from two. It is not the shape or form of a body, which by its nature can be seen with the eyes, heard by the ears, felt by touch, sensed by smell or perceived by taste.* But would you like me to give you a definition of the soul?

Aug.Quant.1,2 (1036); Cassiod. An.3(1287); Rhaban.An.3 (1113B).

JOHN. By all means I wish you to tell me.

AELRED. It seems to me that the soul of man—for this is what I think you are asking about—is, according to the state of our present life, a kind of rational life,* changeable in time but not in place, immortal in its own way,* and capable of being either happy

Aug.Immort. 9,16(1029)
Aug.Ep.166, 2,3(721).

or miserable. By calling it 'rational life', that kind of life is excluded by which trees and beasts live, for they are bereft of reason. By saying that it is changeable in time its nature is shown to be different from that of God, which is changed neither by place nor time. By saying that it is immortal in its own way we exclude that immortality which the holy apostle tells us belongs only to God. For, when speaking of God, he says: 'Who alone possesses immortality'.* And the reason he says this is, because God is always the same and in the same state. This cannot be said of the soul which is drawn here and there by divers desires and wishes.

1 Tim 6:16

JOHN. What do you mean? Are we to believe that the heavenly spirits, who suffer these changes in desires, are not sharers of this immortality?

AELRED. You did well to say 'sharers'. They certainly share in his immortality, that is, his unchangeableness, but they are not immortality or unchangeableness itself. But God is immortal and unchangeable in such a way as to be his own immortality and unchangeableness. He has it from his own nature: the heavenly spirits have it by sharing through grace.

JOHN. Since enough has been said on this point, proceed to the explanation of what follows.

AELRED. In the definition of the soul were added the words 'and capable of being either happy or miserable', in order to exclude the angels, who cannot be miserable, and the devils, who cannot be happy.

JOHN. You say that the soul is life. But even though I should like to, I cannot think what life is.

AELRED. I know the reason for this. You think you cannot have an idea of anything unless you use corporeal images, which you have either perceived with your senses or built up in your imagination.* Therefore, just as when you are thinking of a man you have seen, you set up his image before you, so when you try to think of life you look for its image and believe that there is no substance unless it has a certain form in the memory. Therefore, in wishing to think of life you look for its image in your mind,* and because you do not find it you are disturbed. And yet without using any form or corporeal image you think of many things which are more important than bodies. For when you think of the virtues you do not gaze upon the image of any of them. When, therefore, you consider and turn over in your mind* what light, what knowledge, what consolation, what grace wisdom bestows on human minds,* how much are you moved, how much do you desire to enjoy a share of it, being stimulated to this by Sacred Scripture, which says, 'Seek wisdom and God will give it to you'.* Therefore, what you think of and desire without any corporeal image is greater than and superior to any body.

*Aug.Gen.10,24, 40 (426).

*animus

*mens

*mens

*Si 1:33

JOHN. But I think that wisdom and justice. are accidents, whereas that life of which you speak, that is to say the soul, you call a substance. But how can anyone conceive of a substance without any form or shape?

AELRED. Tell me now, how do you conceive justice?

JOHN. I conceive justice to be a virtue, by which each one is given what belongs to him.* Then I think of what I ought to give God, to my neighbour and to myself. And when I think of the usefulness and pleasure its possession confers, my desire for it is kindled and excited.

AELRED. Why do you not think of life in the same way?

JOHN. I do not know.

AELRED. Consider life as a certain nature that can move, which by a kind of movement gives growth to creatures bereft of sense. This movement is present in trees and herbs, so that sap is led to the root and thence diffused through all parts of the tree, bestowing a kind of life on it, with the result that it becomes green, grows, is covered with leaves, adorned with flowers and becomes heavy with fruit.*

JOHN. I would like to know whether this life is a body or a spirit, or something else which is neither body nor spirit.

AELRED. In no way would I call it a spirit, except in a metaphorical sense, just as air, wind and other things of this kind are called spirits.* However, as all bodies are composed of four well-known elements, so in the nature of the tree these four elements are combined by the wisdom of the Creator in such a way that by the force of air and fire, which are of a more subtle nature than the rest and are better prepared for promoting action than for receiving it,* internal movement is carried

*Cicero, Off.1,6, 21(11);Aug. Lib.arb.1,13,27 (1235).

*Aug.Gen.7,16, 22(363).

*Ibid.30(366); Cassiod.An.1 (1282D);Rhaban, An.1(1110C).

*Aug.Gen.7,19, 25(364).

out and thrives. I do not think, therefore, that this sort of life or movement is altogether immaterial, because its functioning depends upon material elements, even though they are extremely subtle. But just as the elements, by whose force life is procured for the others, are closer to spirit, so indeed is that movement more subtle than the one that is caused by external force. Does this explanation satisfy you?

JOHN. For the present, yes.

AELRED. Now let us give our attention to that life which not only relates to the growth of a body, but also produces a certain spontaneous movement which is linked to sense for the control of the body, as happens in all animals.* That life expresses itself in touch, with the result that it can feel hot and cold, hard and soft, light and heavy, rough and smooth. Then, by seeing, smelling, tasting and hearing it feels and perceives different kinds of colors, shapes, scents, tastes and sounds, seeking out those that are compatible and avoiding those that are disagreeable. At times this kind of life deserts the senses for a short period, and whilst giving their activity a rest, as it were, ponders over the images of objects that it has received through them one after the other and in a number of ways. This we call sleep or dreaming.* That this is the nature of the brute soul has often been observed from the twitching and barking of dogs and from the whinnying of horses.* By the sensual appetite it is impelled towards many things either for pleasure, for need or for affection: for pleasure, as regards coitus;

*Ibid.*17,22*(363).

*Aug.*Quant.*33,71 (1074).

*Aug.*Ep.Man.*17, 20*(185).

*affectus

for need, as regards food and drink; for affection,* as regards the preserving, feeding, fostering and protecting of offspring,* the seeking out of cover, the making of nests and the ingenious preparation of places suitable for their operations. All these things are implanted and impressed on the animal soul by habit, senses, and affection, so that they become part of the memory. The result is that out of a hundred nests, all looking alike, a bird will find its own without mistake, and out of a hundred cells in the hive the bee will find its own.* Sacred Scripture calls this life the spirit of life,† which, because it is bereft of reason, is far removed from rational life. Rational life uses and abuses all these things not only according to its ability but also according to its will.*

JOHN. I would like to know whether you would call this spirit corporeal or incorporeal, mortal or immortal.

AELRED. Saint Jerome says that the brute soul is produced with the body and will perish with the body.* Saint Gregory also says that God created three vital spirits: one which is not clothed with flesh, like that of the angels; one which is clothed with flesh but which will not die, like that of men; and another which is clothed with flesh and will die with it, like that of brutes.* And Augustine, that man of inimitable subtlety, making use of the theories of physicians, says that the movement and sense which we perceive in animals, arises from the element of air or fire. 'For although', says he, 'all flesh presents an appearance of earthly solidity, yet it has in it

*Aug.Quant.33.71 (1074)

*Aug.Conf.10,17, 26(790); Mamert, Stat.1,21,1(723). †Gen 7:15.

*Bern.Gra.7.22 (1014B).

*Jer.Ep.37,9(265).

*Greg.Dial. 4,3(231).

some air which is contained in the lungs and which is diffused from the heart through those veins called arteries. It has besides, not only the burning quality of fire, the seat of which lies in the liver and the brain, but also its illuminating quality which, they say, vaporizes the rises to the brain as to the sky of the body, whence rays dart from the eyes. From the brain also as from a central point delicate vessels are led not only to the eyes, but also to the rest of the senses, namely to the ears and nose and palate for hearing, smelling and tasting. The sense of touch, which is present in the whole body, is directed, they say, from the brain through the medulla of the neck and the spinal column, and thence by extremely fine nerves, which make up the sense of touch, is diffused throughout the whole body.'*

*Aug.Gen.7,13,20 (362).Cf.Mamert, Stat.1,17(719B).

If these statements are carefully examined, it is easy to see that since the spirit is created together with the body and dies together with the body, it does not surpass the quality of air or fire in the real body. In comparison with earth or water it could be considered as incorporeal, but in comparison with the rational and truly incorporeal spirit it can be said to be corporeal. Notice how much we have said about that life by which trees live and how much about the life by which beasts live and feel, and all that we have said has been preceded by thought and a certain interior reasoning and judgement. What is it in us that thought out, judged and decided how all this should be said? It is something great, something sublime, something that far

transcends the qualities which we have said
exist in trees and animals. For they can
neither think nor judge, nor can they understand the difference between what is good and
bad nor between what is useful and what
is not.

JOHN. Do beasts and birds not protect
their lives, as far as they are able, by taking
to flight and hiding under cover? Do they not
take care for their health by procuring food
and drink? They have, besides, so great a
power of memory that they appear in great
measure to come very close to knowledge
and reason.

AELRED. None of this is prompted by
reason or knowledge. What causes these actions in them is the power not of judgement
*Aug.*Quant.*27,56* but of sense. For, as Augustine perceived,*
(1067). many beasts surpass us in the power of sense,
and by making sharp use of it in pursuit of the
things they want for food or pleasure they
acquire such ingrained habits as make them
*Ibid.*29,56(1067)*. appear to imitate reason in small measure.*

JOHN. I see now that the whole appearance of knowledge that we marvel at in beasts
is not a matter of clear judgement but of acute
sense. But because you have explained about
the brute soul what is sufficient for the
moment, let our discussion turn to the nature
of the rational soul, which belongs to man, for
which the other matters were a kind of
prelude.

AELRED. As you wish. But keep firmly in
mind what has been said, so that we do not
labor in vain. It will be of great help. First
then—to begin once more—who is it that

thought out the things we have spoken about? Who made the distinction between the life of the tree and the life of animal? Who? None other than myself. And what am I? A man, of course. And look at my body, visible to the eyes, having length and height. It has different limbs and is comely because of the symmetry of the parts. Now who thought all that out or noticed the detail? The body itself, or some part of it, or a limb?

JOHN. Not even a fool would say so.

AELRED. In my body I am aware of that movement which is involved in whatever concerns its growth. Now does that movement help me at all to discover this, or has it any competence in such matters?

JOHN. None at all.

AELRED. Furthermore, I feel that my body possesses senses, to which is linked spontaneous movement for the control of the body. I see with the eyes, hear with the ears, smell with the nostrils, taste with the palate and touch with the hands. Tell me, which of these, do you think, can do those things?

JOHN. Since these are instruments or organs of feeling, who would consider attributing these powers to them, when I would hardly grant them even to the senses?

AELRED. In order to make clear what we are saying, let us examine how far the senses can go. Can sight go beyond seeing bodies and colors? Or can hearing do anything else beyond hearing bodily sounds? Not to press the point any further, what is your opinion about these things?

JOHN. They do nothing but present the

images of those things they have seen or heard and impress them on the memory.

AELRED. And so, when you see something with your eyes and wish to think deeply about it, is the eye any help to thinking about the object once it has been taken away?

JOHN. Not at all. For we think of a thing according to the image of it that we see.

AELRED. Supposing you did not know what justice was, but after certain discussions you learned what justice was, could you not think of justice?

JOHN. I could, certainly.

AELRED. Did listening impress some image of justice on your mind?

JOHN. Not at all. Hearing is of no help to me at all in this kind of reflection. When I wish to think deeply and subtly, all the bodily senses are a hindrance to me and I often close my eyes so that they will not distract me. That is why I find the silence and quiet of the night so pleasing.

AELRED. Since, therefore, those matters which I have spoken of were not thought out by any limb of the body, or by the senses, or by any instrument of the senses, and I, a man made up of body and soul, did it without the assistance of any of these, the conclusion is that the thinking was done by the soul.

JOHN. Nothing could be more true.

AELRED. Now try as far as you are able to put aside all bodily sense and concentrate all your attention on that power which thinks and look closely at yourself thinking. Suppose that you are in the dark, that you have closed your eyes and stopped up your ears, that your nostrils smell nothing, that your palate tastes nothing and that you feel nothing. Now turn your attention to what it is that, when all these senses are quiet, thinks of so many things, reflects on so many things, proposes and decides so many things, turns over so many questions and makes such clear judgements on many opinions.* It is something great and sublime. When, therefore, you are aware of your soul thinking so strongly, are you aware of any place in which it might be, or of any bodily mass that constitutes it?

Aug.Conf.10,8,14 (785).

JOHN. Not at all. And already I can almost understand that the soul is incorporeal, for although it may reside in the body, I cannot assign to it any particular place in the body.

AELRED. And so you see how simple it is, how destitute of parts and how, in spite of the fact that it lacks length and breadth and height it thinks of so many and such sublime matters without the assistance of any organ of the body and passes judgement on them.

JOHN. I see and I am absolutely delighted.

AELRED. Since, then, the soul exists, lives and thinks, who can doubt that it is a substance?

JOHN. No one, surely.

AELRED. As, therefore, it is a substance lacking length, breadth and height, and you are unable to point out any particular place where it might be, and you are aware of it thinking, but are not able to feel in what part of the body it is residing, would you deny that it is an incorporeal substance?

JOHN. By no means.

AELRED. Now drive away from your

inner gaze all phantasms, all bodily shapes
and the images of all corporeal things, and
ponder on the nature of incorporeal sub-
*Ibid.*12(784) stance.* And first of all I would like you to
tell me whether the soul can think, deliberate,
count and divide without the aid of the
memory.

JOHN. No, it cannot.

AELRED. What? Can it do it then without
the reason?

JOHN. How can there be any doubt about
it, since to judge between what is just and
what is unjust cannot be done without
*Bern,*Div.*45,2
(677D). the reason?*

AELRED. Thinking over these matters
quietly to yourself and examining them carefully, can it do it without the will?

JOHN. This is impossible.

AELRED. These three, then, the memory,
reason, and will, constitute the soul or are
*Bern.*Conv.9(841) certainly present in the soul.*

JOHN. I would more willingly say that
they are in the soul.

AELRED. Would you? Are they there as
parts in the whole, or as accidents in a
substance?

JOHN. I prefer the latter alternative.

AELRED. If these three are accidents of
the soul, they can be separated from the
soul while its substance remains.

JOHN. Not necessarily. Many accidents are
inseparable and cannot be taken away from
their subject.

AELRED. I am not asking you to consult
your eyes or your hands or your ears, but
your reason, of which you are speaking. Is

there any accident which cannot be separated from its subject either actually or in your mind?

JOHN. Perhaps there is, but it escapes me.

AELRED. Now pay attention to this. Are a subject and its accident identical, or is there some difference between them?

JOHN. Indeed, there is a great difference.

AELRED. Can you think of each one separately?

JOHN. Nothing could be easier.

AELRED. Now see whether, when you are thinking of the soul, you can distinguish in the same way between the soul and the reason.

JOHN. Why should I not be able to do so?

AELRED. Look more carefully. How can you think of the soul of a man without its reason (for that is what we are talking about), since, as soon as you begin to think of it without its reason, you cease to think of a soul of a man?

JOHN. If I want to think of a soul that is wise, can I not think separately of the soul on one hand and of its wisdom on the other?

AELRED. What could be more obvious? But the matter we are talking about is far different. A soul that is wise can lose its wisdom and become foolish. Consequently, they can be thought of separately, for although the soul may cease to be wise, it does not cease to be a soul. But you cannot think of a soul as being a soul, unless you think of it as being rational. So these three faculties without which the substance of the soul cannot exist, cannot be called accidents of the soul. Since, then, they are not accidents, the conclusion must be that they are substance.*

JOHN. What I would like to know is, whether they are the substance of the soul or another substance?

AELRED. They are not a different substance. Although they can be separated from one another in thought, it is quite clear to me that these three—memory, reason, and will—are one substance. For though each of them may seem to possess individual powers, they cannot act separately, nor can they be separated from each other. The memory can do nothing without the reason and the will; the reason can do nothing without the will and the memory, and the will can do nothing without the memory and the reason. And so, although the memory is not the reason or the will, and vice versa, these three are one substance and one soul.

JOHN. But Saint Augustine appears to hold an opinion contrary to this. He says 'The soul is one thing, the reason is another. Yet the reason is in the soul and the soul is one. But the soul does one thing, and the reason does another. The soul lives, the reason knows, and to the soul belongs life while to the reason belongs wisdom. And as they are one, the soul alone receives life, and the reason alone receives wisdom.'*

AELRED. This opinion of the saintly father, I think, rather confirms than weakens our statement or assertion. When he openly says that the soul and the reason are one, he clearly wishes the substance of both to be one. And what he said above—that the soul is one thing and the reason another—is not, I think,

contrary to our assertion, and this can be
proved quite easily from the similitude he was
using. For, pay attention to the matter for
the understanding of which he employed this
similitude. The preceding words were: 'God
the Father is one. God the Son is one. God
the Holy Spirit is one. They are not three
Gods, but one God, three in name, but one in
the substance of Godhead.' And lest this
teaching should appear absurd to the heretics
with whom he was arguing, he proved that he
was not talking nonsense about the Trinity by
drawing attention to that creature which is
made in the image of the Trinity. 'For', said
he, 'the soul is one thing, the reason is another.' This is one thing, this is another. Two
in name, but one in substance. The word 'soul'
means one thing to me, the word 'reason'
means something else. For concerning one and
the same substance, which is the soul and
reason, the word 'soul' expresses the idea that
it lives, the word 'reason' that it analyzes. As
for his saying that 'the soul alone receives life,
and the reason alone receives wisdom' it is to
be understood that life has particular regard
to the word 'soul', and wisdom to the word
'reason', because the reason is able to know
wisdom. Nevertheless there is one life of both
and there is one wisdom of both.

JOHN. I am still troubled by what I remember your having said, namely, that the soul
and the reason cannot be separated even in
thought, nor can one be thought of without
the other. Yet look how many things we have
thought about each one, particularly that
statement of Saint Augustine, saying that

the soul was one thing and the reason another, attributing individual powers to each one.

AELRED. It seems to me that your grasp of what we have been saying is superficial. It is one thing to think about the soul and another thing to think of the soul itself; it is one thing to think about the reason and another thing to think of reason itself. We can think of each one separately according to the different meaning of the words, but we cannot think of them separately when it is a question of the identity of their substance. It is not at all possible to think of the human soul without including reason, that is, of a soul that does not possess reason, just as you cannot think of a man who is not a rational and mortal animal.*

*Aug.Ord.2,11,31 (1009);Boeth. Porphy.1(37A).

JOHN. Tell me, please, whether the reason that is in me is different from the one that is in you, and whether individual men have individual reasons. I would also like to know the same about memory and will.

AELRED. I am astonished that you should ask such a question, when you see one man with a retentive memory, another one who is very forgetful, one who is quickwitted and another so dull that he almost seems to have no reason at all, and so many conflicting wills among men.

JOHN. You are pretending not to have understood fully what I said. I thought of asking, not about the strength or weakness of reason and the other faculties, but about the nature of reason, from which a man is called rational: whether reason, by which we are all rational, is one for all men, or whether each man has his own.

AELRED. I knew the direction in which
you were driving me, but desist, I pray you. It
is a fathomless abyss. Even if there is someone
who is able to explain it, there is hardly anyone who understands it. For if I say that there
is only one reason for all men, you will be
prepared to infer that there is only one soul
for all. And if I say that each man has his
own, perhaps I shall be unable to explain how
it is that there is one reason by which I see
that truth should be preferred to falsehood,
and another by which you ponder over the
same things. That is why Saint Augustine
prevented the boy Adeodatus from pursuing
this inquiry, when he asked about the number
of souls: 'I do not know what answer to make
to you. For if I say that there is one soul, you
will be troubled because in one person it is
happy and in another miserable, nor can one
soul be happy and miserable at the same
time. But if I should say that it is one and
many at the same time, I should not know
how to suppress your laughter. If I were to
say that there are many, I should laugh at
myself and bear with less equanimity my own
displeasure than yours. But what is perhaps
an insupportable burden either to both of us
or to one do not impose or try to bear.'*   *Aug.Quant.32,69
(1073).*

JOHN. What is all this? He appears to hold
that there is either one soul, or many and one.
Who can put up with this?

AELRED. Don't get excited. At Jerusalem,
when there was a great multitude of believers,
although each individual had his own soul, it
was said that 'In the multitude of believers

*Ac 4:32. Cf.
Greg.Ep.65.*

there was one heart and one soul'.* Let us, if
you wish, get out of this difficulty by accepting this simple statement, although perhaps it
could be said that in some way there is one
soul because we all share the same rational
nature. Because some people use it well and
others abuse it wickedly they are punished or
rewarded accordingly. But whatever the ob-
scurity of this problem, cling tenaciously to
what has been proved above: that the soul is a
simple being, which is not made up of any
parts and which, because it cannot be divided
nor increased, is neither greater nor lesser in
its substance. Hence there is nothing in its
substance which is not itself. And so, reason,
memory and will, even though they have a
plurality of names and individual powers, are
nothing else in the soul than the substance of
the soul itself.

JOHN. I beg you not to defer a fuller and
wider discussion of the powers and individual
qualities of these three.

AELRED. Why, I ask you, should we be
burdened with a long discussion, when what
you demand can be explained in a few words?
Listen briefly, then. Whatever is seen by the
eyes, whatever is heard by the ears, whatever
is smelled by the nose, whatever is touched by
the hands, whatever is tasted by the palate is
presented to the memory. On all of them
reason passes judgement and the will consents.
Does that satisfy you?

JOHN. Not at all. There are many things
which are commended to the memory or
retained by it, which have not been deposited
there by any of the bodily senses, such as the

theory of numbers, weights and measures and innumerable other things.* So I would like to know what the soul does in the flesh, what in the senses, what through the senses, what does it do in itself through the senses and what without any assistance from the senses.

Aug.Conf.10,12, 19(787).

AELRED. This is a very heavy load. Nevertheless, I will try my best and hope that it will not be useless.

I will use either the words or the sense or both of Saint Augustine, who said: 'The soul, as anyone can easily see, gives life by its presence to this earthly and mortal flesh; it holds all its parts together and keeps them one and does not allow it to dissolve or waste away. It causes all nourishment to be distributed equally between the members, preserves its symmetry and measure not only as regards beauty but also as regards growth and reproduction.'* You see what that wisest of men had to say about the operation of the soul on the flesh or body, adding that man had all these things in common with the animals, since we observe and accept that they, in their kind, live and are preserved and grow.

Aug.Quant.33,70 (1074);Cassiod. An.(1284).

JOHN. Would you say that these actions are to be attributed to the rational soul, since in them sense plays no part, and much less memory, reason and will? Are they not rather to be ascribed to that movement through which trees are said to live and grow?

AELRED. Do you think that sense exists in any body which happens to lack this movement?

JOHN. I certainly would not say that. For the power of sense cannot be where there is no power of existence.

AELRED. Now let us pass from inferior to superior beings. The body of beasts is certainly sown by a seed when male and female mate together. When, therefore, conception follows, that seed is not said to live immediately, because it cannot feel. Soon, however, it has within it that movement, by which it is impelled to take shape and grow. For just as the seed of a tree, planted by nature in the womb of the earth, takes shape by reason of the aforesaid movement and grows and spreads out its branches, so the seed of the beast, infused into the womb of the female, is by the same movement moulded into shape, grows and develops into limbs. Nevertheless, we do not say of it, as we do of trees, that it is alive, because there is another more important life which has to be awaited. But when this life has been added to it, we do not say that there are two lives or two souls in it, but only one possessing a twofold power, one of which lies in the natural movement, by which it becomes a body and lives and grows, and the other of which lies in the spontaneous movement attached to the senses by which it also feels.

JOHN. Is not the human body conceived in the same way?

AELRED. From the fact that 'man has been compared to senseless beasts and been made like them', the condition of both as regards conception and growth is practically the same.

JOHN. Where then does the rational soul come from?

AELRED. You ask the question as if, at some time, man had an irrational soul.

JOHN. Is the human body not first conceived, then formed and increased by a certain internal movement and after a fixed period endowed with sense, at which time it is said for the first time to live?

AELRED. That is what we agreed on a short time ago.

JOHN. How and when, therefore, is the rational soul infused into it?

AELRED. In no way can the human body live without a rational soul. Therefore, without any interval of time, even momentary, as soon as the body begins to live, it begins to have a rational soul and to be a man, that is to say, a rational mortal animal. It did not have at first an irrational soul, such as the one in beasts, which is produced with the body and will die with the body, and afterwards a rational soul, so that it might be said to have two souls. But as soon as it began to live, it began to have a rational and not a brute soul. Some heretics,* not paying heed to this, used to say that Our Saviour took upon himself flesh without a rational soul, not realizing that they were affirming nothing else than that the Word of God became not man, who is never without a rational soul, but a kind of irrational beast.

*Apollinarists. Cf. Aug.Joan.23,6 (1585).

JOHN. Can the rational soul not exist in the body without these senses?

AELRED. By no manner of means. For just as we said a little earlier that no body can be endowed with sense without having that movement which is more subtle than the body and which provides all bodies with growth, so the rational soul cannot unite with this body made up of the coarser and unresponsive elements of earth and water except through the power of sense, which the body has from the elements of air and fire. This power is so subtle and so akin to spirit that it is almost a spirit and is often called, because of its subtlety, the spirit or the spirit of life. Therefore, the Word of God, in comparison with whom all things may in some manner be called corporeal, could in no way be united with flesh and constitute with it one person except through the medium of that nature which is subtler than all the rest and nearer to the divine nature, I mean the rational spirit. Hence, Saint Augustine addressing God the Father, said, 'I knew that flesh did not unite with your Word except with a soul and a human mind*'.

But let us return to our discussion. Although the rational soul makes use of that natural movement which is concerned with growth, the soul is not identified with that movement; and although it employs the power of sense for many things connected with the five senses, yet the soul is not that power of sense or any of the sense organs, as we have shown above.

JOHN. Tell me, I beg you, what you think about the origin of the soul and where it comes from into the body, for you have said enough as regards when it comes.

AELRED. I do not wish to involve myself in this question, which Saint Augustine left unsolved, namely, whether the soul is infused by traduction or whether new souls are created every day. That most eminent Doctor after placing before himself both these opinions and piling up all the reasons and authorities which seemed valid for or against each one, concluded his discussion with these words: 'Having dealt with all these matters as far as time would allow, I would be prepared to declare that the weight of reasons and authorities on both sides were equal or almost equal, were it not that the opinion of those, who were influenced by the baptism of infants and who think that their souls are created by their parents, outweighs the others.'* These are his words. But I would like you to know this; that those who affirm that the soul is infused by traduction* in such a way that it is prepared and produced with the body and that in regard to its substance it receives more and less are in error, and I would not say that about the rational soul at all. But those who hold that the soul is infused by traduction because the power of sense, without which the soul cannot be kept united to the body, draws its matter from the body because of fire and air, both of which are latent in the human seed, are not saying anything too unreasonable, provided the word 'traduction' can be made to fit this opinion. Perhaps you could think of the soul as being infused by traduction, if you could think of sense as something midway between flesh and soul. Because of its nature, which is akin and nearer to spirit, it has in some way a capacity for holding the soul and is like a glue by which the soul is joined to the body and

*Aug.Gen.10,23, 39(426).

*By biological generation.

held in the body, so that the power of matter, latent in the seed, which later develops into sense, is capable of receiving power of a higher order. This power, which flows invisibly and incorporally from the love of the father and mother, lies preserved in the seed and in time passes into the nature of the soul. For in the seed of the body there is an invisible force, immaterial and intangible, which can clearly be distinguished, not by sight or touch, but only by the intellect, from that material of the seed which is recognized by sight and touch.* If anyone, therefore, can think of the soul as having from this power, which is so subtle, some power which is even more subtle and which provides it with the matter or the source of its creation,* then let him, as I said, hold that the soul is infused by traduction.

Aug.Gen.10,21, 37(425).

Ibid.7,6,9(359).

JOHN. I must confess that all this is unclear to me, and I hope that I shall not seem a nuisance to you, if I ask you to repeat it in simpler and more easily understood terms.

AELRED. I will not deny your wish. But pay attention not only to what will be said, but keep in mind what we have discussed. First of all tell me if you are aware that you are alive.

JOHN. Even a sceptic would not deny that.

AELRED. Tell me if you doubt that you can feel.

JOHN. Not at all, for I see with my eyes, hear with my ears and have possession of my other senses.

AELRED. Would you say that the seed of the human body feels and lives immediately once it has been conceived after the congress of male and female?

JOHN. I don't think there is anyone who would say that.

AELRED. What makes it live and feel afterwards? Answer me.

JOHN. As there is no hardness in the seed, how does it get teeth and bones later on?

AELRED. Tell me what you think.

JOHN. I think there is some hidden force within it, from which the body grows and takes shape, which becomes hard in the bones, becomes fat in the flesh, and becomes fluid in the blood.

AELRED. As there is no sense in that seed, do you not understand that there is in it some force or power, by which at a suitable time it lives and feels, sees with the eyes, hears with the ears, and smells with the nose?

JOHN. I see nothing more certain.

AELRED. Did any of the senses help you to see this?

JOHN. None, unless perhaps it was hearing you argue.

AELRED. What then? You certainly heard me arguing, but was it by hearing that you recognized that I was speaking the truth?

JOHN. I acknowledge that this was done not by the power of sense but by the power of reason.

AELRED. Nothing could be more true. Now tell me whether you know you possess a rational soul.

JOHN. Of course I know and understand, and none of the senses helped me to understand. But from the fact that I think, that I discuss, that I judge, that I see, I have no doubts that I possess a rational soul.

AELRED. Splendid. And so you would say that in the seed of which we are speaking there is no rational soul at all.

JOHN. No. I would not say that it either lived or felt. The rational soul is more subtle than any sense. Nor can the soul on account of its subtlety be held in the body because of its materiality, except through the medium of some nature which has both an affinity with the soul because of its subtlety and an affinity with the body because of its bodily quality.*

*Ibid.20,26(365).

AELRED. Very true. I am very pleased that you have not forgotten what was proved a little earlier on. Now see if perhaps you can understand that just as the power lies latent in the seed and although it is not a sense yet later on develops into a sense by means of which the rational soul is held within the body, so, by means of the same force or power another one, more subtle and even more powerful, issuing not from the flesh of the parents but emanating invisibly and incorporeally from their affection, resides in the seed; and this force or power, although it is not the rational soul, is nevertheless the material or source of its creation. I believe that you now grasp what I was trying to tell you a little earlier, when you complained that I spoke obscurely.

JOHN. That is true. But I do not regret being troublesome, since it has borne good fruit.

AELRED. If, therefore, the foregoing can fittingly be applied in word or thought to the soul, one might say, without appearing too foolish, that the soul comes from traduction. This is put forward not as an affirmation, but rather as a question or an opinion, so that you may please yourself whether you doubt it all or remain satisfied with this opinion or join the majority in stating firmly that the soul is not from traduction. For, as far as written authorities are concerned, Saint Augustine declared that the opinions of both sides were equal, except that the argument for traduction taken from the baptism of infants carried more weight.* However, whatever opinion you choose, take care to avoid the impiety of those who in defiance of catholic belief and church order say that the sacrament of Christ is not necessary for infants, for the Apostle openly says: 'By one man sin entered the world and by sin, death. And so death came upon all men, because in him they all sinned.'* For if, they argue, the soul does not come by traduction, how could they have sinned in the person of Adam, with whom they are related only according to the flesh, which cannot sin without the soul? And if God creates new souls every day, God forbid that he should create them sinners.* Since, therefore, the flesh cannot sin before it receives the soul, nor the soul before it becomes clothed in flesh, you must admit either that an infant is immune from original sin or that God is the cause of its perdition. All catholics who have said that the soul is not infused by traduction confess that this problem is insoluble, but they still hold on to their opinion while deploring the heretics'

*Ibid.*10,23,39* (426)*.

**Rom 5:12*

**Aug.Ep.190,6, 24(866)*.

blasphemy. This had to be mentioned, because some foolish and illiterate weavers of both sexes are trying to reinstate this unholy heresy, which was condemned and consigned to oblivion by the holy fathers, and are attempting to overturn all the sacraments of the church with an obstinacy of mind and a *The Albigenses.* contempt for death that is quite irrational.*

JOHN. I have heard that many of them have been cast into prison and that the king *The Council of* has summoned a council* in order to discuss *Oxford, sum-* with his advisers what should be done with *moned in* them, for they condemn marriage, ridicule *1165–6* the sacrament of the altar, deny the resurrec- *Henry II.* tion of the body and preach the uselessness of baptism.

AELRED. Did the Apostle not long ago *Ac 20:29* foretell that such men would arise?* But since it is by these three sacraments that not only the soul but the body also is sanctified and by these mysteries is prepared for future glory, is it to be wondered at that they who deny the resurrection of the body would also deny the sanctification of the body? That is the reason, it seems to me, why they condemn marriage, because they want to have in common all the women who belong to their sect; they consider that depraved actions committed either through or in the flesh are not sins and are not therefore to be detested: they only avoid, as they say, sins of the soul.

JOHN. What I think is most surprising is that they do not fear to suffer death for such errors.

AELRED. As they do not believe in the resurrection of the body, perhaps they have

been convinced by the devil of uncleanness
that the body is their prison, promising them
untold joys when they shall have been delivered from this dungeon. For even the
philosophers promised themselves such happiness after death that not only did they spurn
death, but thought it a worthy act to court it.
Hence it happened that, while one of them was
describing the advantage of death, a member
of his audience, inflamed with the desire of
experiencing it, threw himself from a wall
and perished.*

*Cicero,Tusc.1,34,
84(260).*

JOHN. I wish you could have made acquaintance with that whole sect, so that you
could have persuaded them of the truth.

AELRED. If all the baseness of that heresy
had been brought into the light of day there
would certainly have been no need for anyone
to persuade them, for it would have turned
the hatred of the whole world against them by
its own error. But let us return to our discussion, and tell me what else you wish to hear
about the soul.

JOHN. Before we pass on to something
else, I would like you to give me a summary
of what has been said.

AELRED. As you please. We have said that
the soul is incorporeal, because it was not
created from any corporeal matter or from
the mingling together of bodies. For that
reason it lacks length, breadth and height, and
so we said that it is a simple nature without
parts which, while existing in the body, is not
located anywhere. Hence it is whole in the
whole body and whole in each of the senses,
and when it thinks of itself as thinking, it

cannot think of itself as existing in any place.
In order to make this clearer, we discussed at
length the three modes of life and movement.
But since the soul is of such great subtlety, we
said that it could in no wise be mingled with
the body and that it constituted a person with
the body only through the medium of sense.
Sense arose from the subtle elements of air
and fire, which had been refined and made
fluid, and though it could not be a spirit, it
was capable of receiving the spirit as long as
it existed in man, since in it and through it, as
by an instrument, the rational spirit could
carry out many activities. But although the
soul is not sense, nor is the sense the soul, yet
there can be no sense in the human body
without the soul, nor can there be a soul
without the sense. For as soon as a man begins
to live, he begins to have a human soul and to
be a rational and mortal animal. But since the
soul has reason, memory and will, these three
are not parts of the soul or its accidents, but
identical with it, that is to say, its very
substance.

When we inquired what kind of activity or
nature the soul exercised in the body we
alighted on the problem of the soul's origin,
and without affirming that the soul comes
from traduction we gave our opinion about
the reason and the manner in which it could
be said to come from traduction, and added
the warning that, though the soul might be
said not to come by traduction, no one should
deny the necessity of baptism for infants. The
point which you queried in the second place,
namely about the activity of the soul in and

through the senses, we explained adequately when we were speaking a little earlier about the spontaneous movement that occurs in beasts, for we possess the power of feeling in common with the birds and the beasts. Then you asked me to explain to you what activity the soul exercises in itself through the senses. My short answer is, nothing.

JOHN. How can that be, I ask, when the soul can think of nothing corporeal which has not had its image brought in by the senses?

AELRED. But when the senses have brought it in, do you not think about it with your eyes closed? If so, then whatever the soul does within itself, it does without the assistance of any of the senses.

JOHN. And what is that? Now I recall that this was the last question I put.

AELRED. I recall it too. But if you do not mind, let this be the end of our discussion, so that when our minds have been refreshed somewhat by a period of quiet, we can take up with greater ease the investigation of your queries.

JOHN. As you wish. There is one thing, however, that I would like you to answer. As sense without reason exists in the body of beasts, and there is a great difference between the rational soul and bodily sense, can the soul be separated from it while sense still remains in the human body?

AELRED. I cannot possibly give you a satisfactory answer to this question in so short a time, since it is difficult to explore the way in which the soul sees many things through and in the body, many things in the body but not by the medium of the body, and many things outside the body. But a fuller declaration of all these matters will be made when we deal with the departure of the soul from the body, if he, in whose hands both we and our words remain, will deign to reveal it to us.

JOHN. May God give you discernment to understand, eloquence to express and power to convince. So be it.

END OF BOOK ONE

BOOK TWO

JOHN. It is now time to discuss today those points which we deferred dealing with yesterday.

AELRED. I wish my aptitude for the task was on a par with my desire. The question to be asked is this: what can the soul, without the assistance of the senses, accomplish in itself and by itself through the memory, reason and will?

JOHN. That is so.

AELRED. First of all, recall to mind what we said about these three faculties, memory, reason and will, namely, that they are the substance of the soul and that even though certain of their activities appear to belong exclusively to one, they are inseparable.

JOHN. I remember that very well. So return to those matters which we have put forward as the subject of our discussion.

AELRED. I think the first point to be discussed should concern the faculty of memory.

JOHN. As you wish.

AELRED. On this power or faculty Saint Augustine has a great deal to say,* and in his explanation he expresses astonishment both at its immensity and at its mystery. For the memory is like a vast hall containing almost countless treasures, namely, the images of different bodily objects which have been carried into it by the senses. In the memory

*Aug.Conf.10,8, 14(785).

71

are stored and separately labelled all those
things that have been borne through its doors
by the eyes, such as colors and the shapes of
things; by the ears, such as every kind of
sound; by the mouth, such as various tastes;
by the nostrils, such as scents; and by the
sense of touch, such as things hard and soft,
Ibid.12-13(784). cold or hot, smooth or rough. All these
animus   things the memory receives, and to the mind
seeking out now one, now another, the mem-
ory presents each one in turn by means of its
own particular image. Certain things come so
readily to hand that they present themselves
to the thinker immediately, but some, even
when other things are being sought for, thrust
themselves forward and are brushed aside
only with difficulty. Some things are hidden
beneath such a deep layer of objects that they
can be retrieved from their dark recesses only
with great mental effort. Others make their
appearance, whenever they are required, in
perfect order. In the memory the heavens, the
earth, the sea, and all the creatures that can be
perceived in them are present to the reflective
mind. Only those things that forgetfulness has
buried in its tomb are removed from its sight.

JOHN. If the soul is incorporeal, how can
it embrace within itself bodily images?

AELRED. Is it your opinion that images of
bodily things are themselves bodies?

JOHN. Not at all. At the same time, I am
surprised that the soul is not a body, when its
extent is such that it contains all those
objects.

AELRED. Certainly it is impossible for a
body of any kind to contain within itself

so many things. But tell me, have you ever looked at your reflection in a mirror?*   *Aug.Quant.5,9 (1040).*

JOHN. Very often.

AELRED. Was the size of your reflection bigger than the measurement of the mirror?

JOHN. Not at all. The reflection was greater or smaller according to the size of the mirror.

AELRED. You see, then, that no image can be greater than the thing on which it is impressed.

JOHN. Yes, I see that. Nothing can be more certain.

AELRED. Do you remember London and how vast it is?* Do you call to mind how the   *Ibid.8(1040).* river Thames flows past it, how Westminster Abbey beautifies its western side, how the enormous Tower stands guard over the east and how Saint Paul's Cathedral rises majestically in the middle?

JOHN. I remember it all and I have forgotten nothing.

AELRED. And how do you remember these things? Is it not because you have seen images of them all in your memory?

JOHN. That is quite true.

AELRED. Now pay attention. Does London appear smaller in your memory than it did to your eyes?

JOHN. Neither larger nor smaller.

AELRED. Very true. You are forced to admit then that your memory, and consequently your soul, is greater than London.

JOHN. Yes, I am bound to admit it, since the image of London is impressed on my memory, and no image can exceed the size of the thing on which it is impressed.

AELRED. If, therefore, you could see at a glance the whole world and all that is contained in it, would not anyone who wished to think of the world see its image in exactly the same size?

JOHN. Yes, clearly.

AELRED. Is there any body or any bodily thing in which the image of the whole world can be depicted without some diminution of its size?

JOHN. Not at all.

AELRED. So your memory is greater than the world, not in material size but in spiritual nature.

JOHN. If the soul is so great, how is it confined to so small a body?

AELRED. From this, in fact, it can be proved quite easily that the soul is not confined within the limits of a small body or contained in a place, for though it may seem to be in a body, it somehow forms and depicts within itself so many and such great images of countless objects. For if you were to see with your eyes thousands of worlds similar to the one we know, the likeness of them all would be impressed on your soul without losing anything of their size. So, in my memory I have at hand the heavens and the earth and the sea and all the information I can gather about them, excepting the things I have forgotten.* Unless I could see them all in my memory with their vast spaces, just as I see them outside me, I should be unable to speak about the heavens or the sea or the stars or the mountains or about anything

*Aug.Conf.10,8, 14(785).

else that I have actually seen or heard others
describing. Now, if we have spoken enough
about this power of the soul which deals in
images, let us pass on to its higher power,
which is concerned not with images but with
real things.

JOHN. What do you mean, may I ask,
by real things?

AELRED. Do you not consider that the
science* of measurement, the skill of disputa-   *scientia
tion and the subtlety of calculating are wonderful things? And what of the theory of
measurement, the countless rules and the
different arts, which pertain either to the
practical side of life or to the knowledge of
truth? All these are present in the memory,
not through any image, but just as they are.
In the same way, the virtues of prudence,
fortitude, and justice, if they are in the soul
at all, are not there in the guise of images, but
in their true selves.

JOHN. How can these enter the mind* if   *mens
they are not introduced there by images
of some kind?

AELRED. It is quite clear, leaving other
things aside, that the science of division and
multiplication has no image in the mind.*   *animus

JOHN. How can my soul gain the knowledge of multiplication except by holding
small objects in my hand and sharing them
out into parts, or if I wish to do this solely by
thinking, by turning over and counting their
images?

AELRED. Let it be so. You have learned,
say, the science* of numbers by counting or   *scientia
multiplying. Do you not think that there is a

difference between the science you have
learned and the words or small objects or
images by which you have learned it?

JOHN. I certainly do.

AELRED. You see then that there is no
image of that science.

JOHN. Yes, I see and I am delighted,
because this is for me a proof that the soul is
incorporeal. In no way can a corporeal object
contain an incorporeal body, nor is any
bodily object capable of possessing wisdom.

AELRED. You have made a good observa-
tion. But as that science has not been seen
by the eye or heard by the ear or smelled by
the nostrils or tasted or touched,* in what
manner or by what entrance did it reach the
soul, so that it resides and is retained there in
such a way that I am able to bring it to mind
whenever I wish and to store it away again
when I like?

JOHN. I do not know how to answer that.

AELRED. When you heard a teacher ex-
plaining the number six and its individual
parts and giving such clear reasons for it that
you accepted the truth of what he had said,
did you simply believe him or see the reason
in your own mind?*

JOHN. Without doubt I recognized as true
in my own mind what I had heard.

AELRED. So perhaps the reason was there
all the time, but you had failed to notice it.

JOHN. It seems likely, then, that what certain secular scholars have accepted is true,
namely, that the natural sciences* reside in
the rational soul. But because the corruptible
body weighs down the soul and the weakness

*Aug.Conf.10,8,
14(787).

*animus

*artes naturales

of the bodily organs dulls the senses, and the images of bodily objects darken and depress the intellect, it is only with great difficulty that they are recalled to the intellect at another's bidding, hidden as they appear to be in the innermost recesses of the memory. So when the mind* does notice them, it realizes that they have not been brought in, as it were, from outside, but are implanted by nature.

Seneca,Ben. 4,6(90).

AELRED. This opinion appears from the book of the *Confessions* to have the approval of Saint Augustine. But because there is difficulty in providing a convincing proof for it, let us move forward to the discussion of other things. Now the memory has one supreme quality that overrides all else: it has the capacity of receiving God. From the moment that man knows God, God begins to dwell in his memory, and as often as man brings God to mind, he finds him there.*

Aug.Conf.10,24, 35(794).

JOHN. Is this not common to all men, both good and bad? Am I to say, then, that God dwells in the wicked just because at some time or other, like the good, they remember him?

AELRED. You are aware of what the Apostle said about the wise men of this world, namely, that they knew God, yet they did not glorify Him as God.* So God dwelt in their memories but not in their love. And because they did not give glory to him as God, they have perished. Let what we have said about the faculty of memory suffice, so that we can discuss briefly the faculty of reason.

Rom 1:21

JOHN. Do as you please. Wherever you lead I am prepared to follow.

AELRED. We have shown that reason

belongs to the substance of the soul. The power of reason is so great that it distinguishes us from the rest of the animals and by it we are placed above all of them. On it the memory depends so much that it would be able to retain, to distinguish, or to judge nothing except the images conveyed to it through the senses. Yet notice, in spite of the difference in names, how great a unity of nature or substance exists between them. Memory, shorn of reason, certainly does not go beyond the power of an irrational soul, while reason without memory is unable to make anything connect or hang together. In short, memory cannot be conceived without reason or reason without memory, because they are one simple substance.

JOHN. All that pertains to memory, then, pertains to reason. Consequently, memory and reason are one. If that is so, it seems to me that memory is reason, and reason is memory.

AELRED. Certainly reason and memory are one, and they are one soul. Yet reason is not memory, and memory is not reason. For memory signifies one power of the soul and reason another. Memory, in fact, signifies that power by which the soul recalls things and by which it links up sequences of events, connecting those that follow to those that have gone before and those of the future to those of the past. But reason distinguishes between all these and passes judgement on them, approving one as true and another as false, one as just and another as unjust, one as happy and another as unfortunate. Is not this clearer to you than light itself?

JOHN. What else can I say?

AELRED. Good! Now see whether memory can exercise its powers without the aid of reason and whether reason can act without memory.

JOHN. I see and am dumbfounded. For I recognize in the creature what in the Creator is rather to be believed than understood: number without number, plurality in singularity, particularity in unity. For who is unaware that the particular function of the memory is to remember, while that of reason is to distinguish? Yet I am quite unable to conceive how the memory can exist or recall anything without the reason, or how reason can distinguish anything without memory. I see quite clearly the difference in the names and the particular manner in which each undertakes its function, but in substance and in action there is identity. So they are at the same time two and one. There appears to be plurality because they are two, and unity because they are one.

AELRED. It should not now be difficult to understand what we believe, namely that the Trinity in whom we profess our faith is one God and that singularity is adored in the persons, unity in the essence and equality in majesty.

JOHN. What we have proved so far about the soul opens up an easy way to understanding of this reality. Yet proceed with the discussion, which you have begun, on the power of reason.

AELRED. First of all, examine carefully what is done in matters needful for everyday

life. Consider the crafts of artisans, the tilling
of the fields, the building of cities, the manifold wonders of palaces and monuments, the
pictures, sculptures, writings, symbols, the
invention of arts, the institution of laws with
their enactments, rights, diverse judgements in
different cases, and the thousand and one
details of this kind which are thought out by
reason, expressed in decrees, obeyed with
approval, but despised or disregarded at one's
peril. Furthermore, all those things which we
have said are contained in the memory—that
is, the knowledge of divers arts which are implanted by nature in the soul—lay through
weakness in a deep slumber before they were
brought to birth. But as soon as they were
noticed by reason, they were in some way
roused from sleep and thrust into public
view. Even supposing they were elsewhere—in
some kind of fountain to which pupils are led
by their teacher, so that they can gaze upon
them there and thence draw their knowledge—
even so they could not do it without the help
of reason.

JOHN. What kind of fountain, may I ask,
could it be, in which we surmise that all the
arts exist?

AELRED. I believe that supreme Wisdom,
which is God, contains in itself the laws and
sources not only of all the arts, but of all
things, whether they be movements or events.
The closer one approaches it with an un-
blemished eye, the more clearly will one
observe the things contained in it. But no
approach to it is possible without the aid of
reason. It is by reason that we distinguish

truth from falsehood, justice from injustice;
and since reason has a capacity for wisdom, it
is through reason that knowledge of God is
attained.

And take note of the wisdom of the Creator. All the qualities which are common to
birds and beasts and ourselves were bestowed
more generously on them than on us, in order
that the physical attributes in which they are
our superiors should be held by us in low
esteem, compared to those things which make
us superior to them. What man can match the
eagle for sharp vision or the dog for sense of
smell or the peacock for color? What man can
boast the strength possessed by the lion? Who
is as fleet of foot as the goat or as swift in
flight as the fly?* And in order that you may
realize how little power the body or senses
possess in comparison with reason, what man
could evade the snares of even one fly, if that
fly were endowed like man with reason? If the
fly wished otherwise, who could lie in peace
or safely open his eyes? Consider how many
men one poisonous beast could sting if it
possessed reason and could plan an ambush,
the time, the place and the method of attack.
If sparrows and crows had the dictates of
reason to tell them what to do, where to do
it and what precautions to take, how many
cities and castles could they not burn down?
If they enjoyed reason and were equal to men,
could not all the birds and beasts mass together and destroy the human race? Imagine
your own body as having only senses and no
reason, and then you will appreciate how
much better are the bodies of the most

*Cf.Aug.Civ.Dei
8,15,1(240).

despised animals.

Consequently it seems to me that if the human body were not ruled by reason it would be the most abject and wretched of all bodies. Some people, inadvisedly concentrating on this aspect, place such little worth on the body that they do not believe that it will rise again. They fail to distinguish between nature and its defects, between the dignity of creation and the penalty of transgression, between the bliss that has been lost and the corruption that has been incurred. Who is not aware that human bodies were more efficient than the bodies of animals before man was compared to the beasts of the field and became like them?* Yet all the body's weaknesses, all its ills, all its sufferings, even death itself are not wisely used by reason. Notice to what good use the holy patriarch Job put his bodily infirmities.* Look how pleasing a fragrance the dunghill on which he sat, the purulent sores that he scratched, the fetid odor that exuded from his pores, the maggots that covered him have wafted over the whole earth. Herod, on the other hand, put them to wrong use and breathed his last, rotten with worms.*

JOHN. How can anyone make a wrong use of reason, since he can perform an evil act only by going against reason? Anything done with the use of reason is reasonable. But what is reasonably done is rightly done, and what is rightly done is well done.*

AELRED. I certainly agree that no evil act can be done without the use of reason, for a creature bereft of reason can do neither

*Ps 49:12

*Job 2:8

*Ac 12:23

*Aug.Ord.2,11, 31(1009).

good nor ill. We say that an evil act is a sin. But a lion commits no sin when it leaps upon a man and tears him to pieces, nor does a snake sin if it kills a man with its poisonous bite. Consequently only an angel and a man, because they have been created rational beings, can commit sin.

JOHN. I fail to see how a sin can be committed with reason, since every sin is a sin for no other cause than that it is contrary to reason.

AELRED. You are mistaken. You ignore the fact that reason is spoken of in two senses. Reason, according to its nature, is so called because it makes a man rational and makes him able to distinguish between right and wrong. If he could not make this distinction he would be unable to commit sin. Reason is also so called according to its act of judgement, by which it approves of what should be approved and reprehends what should be reprehended. From the nature of reason itself, therefore, it follows that man naturally prefers justice to injustice, chastity to lust. But insofar as judgement is an act of choice, reason suggests that good should be pursued and that evil should be avoided. So whoever commits a sin does so as a result of his nature, which makes him a rational being, because he knows that one thing is good and another bad, but he disregards its judgement in choosing what is bad and spurning what is good.

JOHN. I am not quite clear about what you are saying.

AELRED. How do you know that adultery is evil?

JOHN. For the simple reason that I would not like to be the victim of it.

AELRED. So you know it by reason?

JOHN. Certainly.

AELRED. If you lacked reason, you would not know what adultery was and you would not know that it was evil.

JOHN. That is true.

AELRED. So you would not be able to commit adultery. Everyone knows that animals, who lack reason, cannot commit adultery or fornication because they cannot sin. Without the faculty of reason sin cannot be committed. So, everyone who commits a sin does so because he acts contrary to the dictates and persuasion of reason. Every man who sins acts against reason insofar as its judgement is concerned. Every man who sins acts without reason insofar as its nature is concerned, because by it he is a rational creature.

JOHN. That is enough for me. Let us pass on to the discussion of other things.

AELRED. What things have you in mind?

JOHN. The faculty of the will and the way the soul acts through it.

AELRED. The order of our discussion certainly demands it. Therefore, just as the soul remembers by the memory, distinguishes between things by the reason, so it gives consent by the will.* Since each of these has something proper to itself, they are three in number, but because they have the same substance they are one. And although only the memory remembers, only the reason distinguishes and only the will consents, yet all their operations are inseparable, so that the memory recalls

*Aug.Lib.arb. 3,10,29(1285); Bern.Gra.1,2 (1002B).

nothing without the aid of reason and will, the reason distinguishes nothing without the intervention of memory and will, and the will does not consent without cooperation from reason and memory. These three are one simple substance, not a composite: reason together with memory and will distinguishes; memory together with reason and will remembers; will together with reason and memory consents. So the will is understood in two ways, from the point of view of nature and from the point of view of its inclinations,* that is to say, according to what it is and according to how it is inclined. It is in regard to this latter viewpoint that one judges whether a man is good or bad, just or unjust, wise or foolish. For the will, as regards its nature, is a great good and can never be anything but good. But the use of it, which depends on the way it is inclined, can be good or bad. Therefore, the will, taking it according to its nature, is simply a will, but the right use of it makes it a good will. So the man who pursues good uses this will well, whereas the man who is bent on evil uses his will badly.*

*affectus

*Bern,Gra.4,10 (1007B).

JOHN. I would like you to explain this to me more clearly with examples.

AELRED. Do you not meet hundreds of examples of this? Sight is a good gift of nature and it can never be anything else but good. But to look upon a woman to lust after her is bad and can never be anything else but bad.*

*Mt 5:28

JOHN. As we speak of a good and a bad will, can we speak of sight as good and evil?

AELRED. In the usual manner of speaking

sight refers to that gift by which we see or are able to see even when we are not looking. Its use is commonly called 'a look', and this can be good or evil. It is evil if the look is impure or cruel or full of anger and bitterness or if it expresses contempt or ridicule. It was an impure look that the shameless woman cast upon the youth Joseph, when she enticed him by saying, 'Sleep with me'.* It was an impure look that the old men cast upon the beautiful Susanna and which made them burn with lust for her; and when she resisted, they were furious but finally paid the penalty for lust and falsehood.* And what shall I say of Holofernes, whose impure gaze enslaved him to a woman of wisdom and led to the cutting off of his head?* And who would deny that wicked Ahab's look was cruel as he gazed in triumph on the innocent blood of Naboth? With how deep a look of anger and bitterness Joseph's brothers regarded him as he approached them is made manifest in their words: 'Here comes the dreamer'—this with anger. 'Let us kill him'—this with bitterness. 'Let us see what his dreams are worth'—this in ridicule.* All these people abused a good gift of nature, which remained good, to their own damnation. But the man who makes good use of the gift of nature, who regards the poor and indigent with a kindly eye to show pity on them,* or who gazes intently on the cross to feel compassion, or who diligently pores over the pages of Sacred Scripture to gain instruction, he acquires merit for himself. In the same way, the will is a natural good which, if used by man for sin and for the

*Gen 39:8

*Dan 13:8

*Jdth 10:17

*1 Kg 21:16

*Gen 37:19-20

*Ps 41:1

desire of sinning, becomes by its evil use an evil will.

JOHN. I gladly accept this distinction, which was unknown to me before. It makes clear to me that the power of the will is so great that, as far as I can see, the whole worth of a man, good or evil, depends upon it.

AELRED. Very true. But supposing a man did not know how to distinguish between its two uses, how could he know which one to choose?

JOHN. There is no way.

AELRED. How could he distinguish them?

JOHN. Everyone knows that. By reason, surely.

AELRED. You see, then, that in order for a man to act well or ill two faculties must work at the same time, reason and will.

JOHN. Nothing could be more true.

AELRED. That is why, for the purpose of showing that there is one thing in man to which good or bad may be attributed, a word has been formed from these two faculties, reason and will, which is called free-choice. By this one term two things are signified without which there can be no merit either good or bad: namely freedom, which resides in a man's will; and judgment, which belongs to his reason. If either of these is lacking, a man can act neither well nor ill. Just as reason and will are natural goods, therefore, so is free choice, which issues from both of them.* The bad angels misused it and fell: the good angels employed it rightly and kept their place.* The first man also misused it and death followed, whereas the second used it perfectly and

*Aug.Nat.bon. 4,9(551)

*Bern.Gra.4,9 (1007A)

was glorified.

JOHN. Then what does grace do?

AELRED. Not so fast. Since you already know about the judgment of reason, consider for a moment the freedom of the will and thus fuse the properties of each into the one term, free-choice.

JOHN. Nothing would please me better.

AELRED. The rational will is so free that it cannot be compelled to do anything either by man, the devil, an angel or any other creature, for God himself, from the moment he bestowed it, neither took it away, nor increased nor diminished it. So the will can never be forced and nothing can be extorted from it. Apart from the will everything else that belongs to man lacks freedom and consequently is necessarily swayed by the passions. Life, sense, appetite, wit, memory, reason may suffer from some defect, but that defect is not a sin unless it is incurred voluntarily.* For, to name but a few examples, neither a sluggish wit nor a forgetful memory nor an ignorant reason are imputed as sin. Of the will alone can a defect be called a sin, for the will is complete master of itself and lies under no compulsion.

JOHN. How is the will free if it is held captive by iniquity to such an extent that it wants to will many things but is unable to do so?

AELRED. Whatever the will wills to do, it wills to do because it can will. Whatever it does not will and as long as it does not will, then it cannot will, for the simple reason that it does not will. From the moment that it wills

*Ibid.2,5(1004B).

anything, it wills it by an act of the will, and consequently wherever the will is, there can be no compulsion. If you will to go to church, no compulsion can take this will away from you nor can anything else except the will. For if you change your mind and then do not will to go to church, your desire not to go arises not from compulsion but from your own free-choice. So whichever path you take, whether good or bad, the will is there and so is your freedom.*

*Aug.Corrept.14, 43(942).

JOHN. What do you mean? Cannot someone who is stronger than I compel me to go to church?

AELRED. Let us suppose this to be so, although I cannot see how it could happen. Can anyone compel you to go to church? Just see if anyone can force you to go. Certainly you can be dragged there, but who can force you to go?

JOHN. Were many people not forced by torture to deny Christ?

AELRED. You are mistaken. No one denied Christ against his will. Who could force him with any kind of torture to a denial? Picture to yourself a rigorous judge sitting before the tribunal and two prisoners brought into his presence. He eyes them with a menacing glare and a murderous countenance and threatens them with death, with crucifixion, with exposure to wild beasts, with burning and other torments unless they deny Christ. One of them, terrified, gives in: the other stands unmoved. Does the one who stands unmoved do so willingly or unwillingly?

JOHN. No one can doubt that he does

it willingly.

AELRED. And he who denies makes his denial willingly?

JOHN. Certainly, sometimes unwillingly and with sorrow, perhaps even with tears.

AELRED. If one of them could refuse to deny if he wishes, why could not the other?

JOHN. Because one could bear the torture and the other could not.

AELRED. By denying, then, he wishes to avoid torture. Did the judge not give him a choice between denying Christ and having his freedom, between holding to his faith and being tortured?

JOHN. Yes, that is so.

AELRED. So he chose one alternative rather than the other. In this way you see that the will is free on all sides. Join this freedom of will to the judgment of reason and in these two recognize the power or faculty of the rational soul, which is called free-choice. This is able to distinguish between good and evil by the judgment of the reason, and to choose either by the freedom of the will. Look carefully and notice that free-choice, by which the soul is naturally able to distinguish good from evil and to choose whichever of the two it likes, is one thing, but that free-choice by which it actually does it, namely choosing good or evil, is something else. Free-choice, then, is a natural good: the selection of good or evil is the right or wrong use of it.

JOHN. Can, then, a man use free-choice equally for good or evil?

AELRED. He certainly can. Without free-choice he is capable of neither good nor evil.

For that reason it depends upon free-choice whether a man be saved or damned, since no creature that lacks free-choice can be damned or saved.

JOHN. So if I make bad use of my free-choice, that is enough to ensure my damnation, whereas if I use it well, it will ensure my salvation.

AELRED. That is true. But see whether, in order to use it properly, you need the help of anything or whether you can do it for yourself.

JOHN. Why should I not be capable of doing it by myself, since I possess free-choice?

AELRED. A short time ago we distinguished between the nature of free-choice and its use. Would you like me to repeat it?

JOHN. There is no need.

AELRED. So, whether you use it well or not, you will not lack free-choice as long as you have will and reason. I did not say 'a good will or a bad will', but just a will, referring to its nature, not to its use. Free-choice, insofar as its nature is concerned, belongs equally and without difference to God and to every creature both good and bad; and it is not lost or diminished by sin or by suffering, because whether the good man uses it for good or the wicked man for evil, it always remains one and the same in both.* Therefore, whether you are capable of putting it to good use by yourself or need someone else to assist you, you always possess free-choice, which you can use either alone or assisted for good. Hence, it appears to me that sin is nothing else but a wrong use of free-choice, and

*Bern.Gra.*10,35* *(1020A); 4,9* *(1006C).*

goodness is a right use. But as reason and will combine in free-choice, in order to make clearer what we are saying, let us speak of the will from which voluntary consent proceeds (the criterion by which sin is judged), understanding always that reason abides in it. I cannot recall that I have ever encountered this term 'free-choice' in the Scriptures, but only the will which is always accompanied by reason. Since certain irrational animals seem to have a will the word 'free-choice' was invented to express the rational will, which, being under no compulsion, is the sole cause of sin.* It is impossible for the will, of its very nature, not to obey itself, since one cannot will and at the same time not will. The will can certainly be changed, but only into another will, so that at no time does it suffer compulsion.* Consequently, whatever happens to you against your will, such as nocturnal pollution or sexual urges, is attributed more to passivity than to activity. Only when the will is involved in any of these occurrences and gives its consent to the suggestion can there be any question of sin. As a result, neither a sluggish wit, nor a poor memory, nor an unruly appetite nor a dulled sense, nor weak health make man a sinner any more than the contrary things can make him innocent,* for all these matters are out of his control and against his will.

JOHN. If that is so, why is the will incapable of acting by itself?

AELRED. This is a question that remains to be investigated. I believe you are suffi-

Aug.Lib.arb.3, 16,48(1294).

Bern.Gra.2,5 (1004B).

*Ibid.

ciently convinced that whether the will is
able to operate for good by itself or needs
the help of another, the will in its nature
remains free. For if a man were able at any
time to will nothing at all, or to will anything
without the will, then it would be possible for
free-choice not to exist.

JOHN. I accept that as proved to me by
strict reasoning.

AELRED. Now, then, let us look at the
problem which, a little time ago, I thought
should be deferred: whether man needs the
grace of God in order to do good, or whether
the will with its great freedom is self-suffi-
cient.

JOHN. I most earnestly ask you to unravel
this question for me.

AELRED. See to it, then, that you keep
fixed in your memory the two points that
have been established.

JOHN. What are they?

AELRED. The distinction between nature
and use; and the fact that, whether the will
needs assistance or not, it always remains
entire. These points being firmly established,
let us start clarifying what remains obscure.

JOHN. As you wish.

AELRED. First of all let us listen to the
words of Saint Paul: 'To will is within my
power, but how to perform that which is
good I do not find'.* Remember, we said   *Rom 7:18
that wherever the will is mentioned, it means
the will accompanied by reason. 'To will', he
says, 'is within my power.' To will good is not
within my power, but only to will. To will
comes naturally to a man because he has a

will, but to will good or evil is the right or wrong use of the will. Therefore, he said, 'To will is in my power', that is to say, I have a will, I have free-choice by which I can will good; 'but how to perform that good I do not find', because I cannot will good without help. And he spoke correctly in saying 'perform',. for to perform what is good is to will a thing perfectly. What you will perfectly, you do; or, if you are unable physically to do it, you leave it aside. Whatever you will and are unable to carry out, says Saint Augustine, God considers done.*

*Aug.Enarr.57,4 (677).

JOHN. From where, then, does that contradiction arise in my soul, when I seem to wish two opposite things? I often command myself to will what I approve of, but the will does not obey itself.*

*Aug.Conf.8,9,21 (758);Bern.Gra. 2,5(1004B).

AELRED. And what except the will gives the command to will something? If it did not will something, it would not give a command.

JOHN. Well, why does it not carry out what is ordered?

AELRED. Because it does not give an unqualified command. For if the will was entire it would not have to give a command, since the will would be already made up. So, part of it wills and the other part does not will. This is a sickness of the will, which is weighed down by habit and not totally lifted up by truth.* Free-choice, that is, the rational will, is drawn in two opposite directions, so that the nearer it approaches one side, the further it withdraws from the other, until it finally decides on one alternative and thoroughly despises its opposite. 'To perform

*Aug.Conf.8,9,21 (758-9).

the good', he said, 'I do not find'—that is, I
am unable to will perfectly, steadfastly, and
completely while one part is fighting against
the other, one lifting, the other throwing
down. To make this more clear by an example, imagine on one side the reason, led as it
were by the will to approve good, chaste and
honorable things, and on the other side the
appetite, goaded by the flesh and panting
with desire for pleasure. Between these two
the will is dragged in opposite directions, for
reason tells it that good is preferable while
appetite tells it that evil is more pleasurable.
When the will makes a definite choice of one
of these, then it is wholly good or bad and it
will be considered as sinful or righteous.

JOHN. That satisfies me completely.

AELRED. But listen carefully to the rest
that has to be said. Whichever of these two it
chooses, it gives its willing consent.

JOHN. Obviously.

AELRED. Therefore, what it does willingly, it does without compulsion, and what it
does without compulsion, it does without
anyone forcing it.* So, whatever direction it *Aug.Spir.litt.
takes, free-choice, that is the rational will, 31,53(234).
remains intact.

JOHN. I do not think there is any further
doubt about this.

AELRED. Listen to what follows. If an
evil spirit or a wicked man were to approach
the person we were speaking of a little earlier
and, while he was trying to make up his mind,
were to entice him by sensations or sugges-
tions or anything else into giving his consent,
and he began to will fully what he had willed

earlier only in part, would he be willing it less just because he had been persuaded to do so *Aug.*Vera *14,28 (134).* by someone else?*

JOHN. Not at all.

AELRED. So his free-choice has not been impaired?

JOHN. Certainly not.

AELRED. Now turn your attention to the other alternative. Even if a good spirit or an upright man should use every possible means to make a hesitant person will what is good, so that through his urging he gives a willing consent, would that take away his free-choice?

JOHN. No sensible person would say so. But what disturbs me is that the will of itself is quite capable of choosing evil, but in order to choose good it needs the help of grace, without which it cannot attempt the least thing.

AELRED. This is catholic and apostolic belief. But I would like you to tell me whether an angel can or cannot sin.

JOHN. No christian has doubts about it.

AELRED. If, therefore, an angel cannot sin, he remains stable and immoveable in good.

JOHN. That is true.

AELRED. How does he do this, of his own free will or by compulsion?

JOHN. How could he be good, if he were *Ibid.13,26(153).* not good willingly?*

AELRED. Look now. He is freely good to the extent that he is willingly good. For if he is drawn into anything under compulsion, even though what he does appears to be good, he does not perform it as a free agent but as a slave, and for this reason he does not perform

it well. Consequently, if an angel from heaven, who cannot sin, freely remains good, that
is, through his own good ness and not through
any external pressure, he uses his free-choice
so much the more happily the less his will is
allowed to stray from goodness and can neither be forced by anyone nor is actually
forced. In the same way, the devil with equal
freedom fell into sin and persisted in it, not
from any external compulsion but of his own
free will. Consequently, just as the good angel
can do no wrong, so the devil can do no right.
However, because he is evil voluntarily, he
possesses freedom of will, though his mind is
held captive. He can never do good because
he does not will to do good, just as the good
angel cannot sin because he never wills to turn
his will towards evil.*

*Bern.Gra.4,9
(1007).*

JOHN. I am still disturbed by the fact that,
leaving aside the question about the act of
willing which, as we have adequately proved,
is always the same, I can still will evil but am
unable to will good.

AELRED. By what can you will evil?

JOHN. By free-choice.

AELRED. And can you not will good
without free-choice?

JOHN. Not at all.

AELRED. So you have free-choice in
both cases.

JOHN. That is true. But the will is not
capable of willing good by itself, but is
capable of willing evil.

AELRED. Why is it that the will is capable
by itself of willing evil?

JOHN. Because it is free.

AELRED. Does an angel's will lack freedom because it cannot sin? If so, we have labored in vain all day, building up arguments to show that freedom of will exists equally in all rational creatures. How is it that the will can commit sin when there exists a will that cannot sin?

JOHN. I am getting confused by all these questions.

AELRED. Tell me, first, what does committing sin involve?

JOHN. Willing something that one ought not to will.

AELRED. What kind of thing can a man will that he should not?

JOHN. For example, theft, fornication, and adultery—things like that.

AELRED. Now see if in all these things you can think of sin as being anything else than a disregard for the Creator and a desire to make use of some creature contrary to the manner and order laid down by God. The man who wishes to commit fornication—what else does he want but to make use of his own or another person's body against the express law of God? This can easily be observed in adultery, theft and every other kind of illicit pleasure to which the will gives consent. There are others who are not overcome by evil desires but who tell lies or backbite or utter spiteful remarks or foolishly entertain thoughts that God does not exist. Insofar as they make a wrong use of their tongue, their hand or other bodily member they are reasonably considered to be guilty, because lying is preferred to truth, which is a disregard for and an injury to the Creator. A sin may be defined in other words as a spontaneous movement of the will away from the Creator and towards the creature. Consequently, a will is sinful if it disregards the Creator who alone has true being, and consents to make use of something that has lesser being or none at all.

JOHN. What do you mean 'It has none at all'?

AELRED. A lie is nothing; an idol is nothing; a heresy is nothing. Those who think they believe in Father, Son and Holy Spirit, the Father being the greatest, the Son lesser and the Holy Ghost least of all, have turned their faith and their feelings towards nothing for God is not a Trinity like that.*

*Aelred probably had the Sabellian heretics in mind.

JOHN. What sin is has been adequately described, since Saint Augustine taught that all sin is non-being.* Hence it is accepted that a man who commits a sin tends towards non-being. But although I am led by so great an authority to believe this, I am not convinced by reason.

*Aug.Joan.1,13 (1385); Sent.Ans. (70).

AELRED. Let us leave aside this matter for the moment. Note carefully what constitutes an upright will, which is known to be opposed to sin.

JOHN. As you please.

AELRED. An upright will is one that desires to enjoy the Creator for His own sake and the creature for the sake of the Creator.* When this will is so strong and steadfast that it cannot be enticed away to anything else by bodily pleasure, nor be deceived nor led away by falsehood, nor compelled by force, then it can enjoy and rest assured of perfect

*Aug.Doct.3,10,16 (72).

righteousness.

JOHN. This definition of yours satisfies me. But where is all this leading?

AELRED. Do you doubt that God is immutable?

JOHN. May God preserve me from such madness that I should assert or believe that God is changeable.*

Aug.Joan.1,8 (1385).

AELRED. Good. And no one denies that God created all things?

JOHN. That is so.

AELRED. Did he create them from nothing or from some pre-existing matter?

JOHN. It is written that he created everything from shapeless matter.

AELRED. But no one else than he created shapeless matter.* For if another did so, He would not be the Creator of all things. But if He created it, then the same question can be repeated until the conclusion is reached that He created everything from nothing. The question remains, then, whether things were created mutable or immutable. Everyone can see that bodies are subject to change, and everyone is conscious that the soul is also changeable. That angels were created changeable is apparent from the fact that some progressed to a better state and that others lapsed into a worse state. God alone, therefore, is said truly to be, because he is always the same, possessing immortality, that is, immutability, by his very nature and dwelling in inaccessible light.* As he said to Moses: 'I am who am. And he who is, sent me to you'.* Indeed he is in such a way that he is the being of all things, as Denys the Areopagite put it:

Aug.Conf.12,8,8 (829).

1 Tim 6:16

Ex 3:13

'The being of all things that exist is super-
essential Godhead'.* Insofar, therefore, as the
rational will is turned towards him, it moves
towards true being, which is unchangeable.
But in proportion as it turns away from him,
it withdraws from true being and moves
towards non-being. But in order to approach
the unchangeable good, from which it was not
made, but by which it was made, it needs the
assistance of unchangeable goodness itself, by
whose goodness it was made. Nothing that is
changeable can become unchangeable except
by sharing in that goodness which is not
changeable. Now, since the mind cannot of its
very nature do this, because it is changeable,
it can achieve this only by the grace of that
Being which is by nature unchangeable. Freedom of will, however, is in no way affected,
because the only thing that can lapse into a
worse state or rise to a higher is the will, in
which reason together with freedom resides.
Tell me if this satisfies you on this question.

*Ps-Denys,Div.
nom.5,4(818).*

JOHN. There is still one point that I think
should be investigated: whether an angel or a
man, before falling into sin, could have per-
severed in that state of perfection without the
help of a higher being.

AELRED. We gave some attention to this
a little earlier, when we stated that all things
which are by nature changeable cannot per-
severe in good or make progress from bad to
good and from good to better without sharing
in unchangeable good.

JOHN. What fault, then, could be imputed
to angel or man when they fell, if they did
not have that help by which alone they

could remain stable?

AELRED. If they had lacked help, both of them, without question, would have sinned with impunity. But observe these steps, as it were: being able to sin, being able not to sin, not being able not to sin, not being able to sin. In paradise Adam was, by his very nature, able to sin; but with the aid of grace he was able not to sin.* In no way was it possible for him not to sin except by the grace of Him whose nature it is not to be able to sin. Consequently, two things were open to him: the ability to sin; and the grace by which, if he so willed, he could remain without sin. After the fall he became weaker. Already, by his very nature, he could commit sin, but as a result of the corruption of that nature and the just punishment for the crime that had been committed, he was unable not to sin.* From this we hope to be delivered by the grace of God through Our Lord Jesus Christ. It is by this grace that the saints pass through life without grave sin, while those faults which human weakness cannot avoid they redeem by good works and prayers, waiting to reach that state which we know has been attained by the angels, namely, the inability through God's grace to incur or to fear sin.

Let these remarks about the nature of the soul as regards memory, reason and will suffice for the present. But if there is any further question concerning the soul which you think should be discussed, do not hesitate to ask it.

JOHN. There are, indeed, a number of questions that occur to me, but particularly regarding the immortality of the soul.

*Aug.Corrept.12, 33(936).

*Bern.Gra.7,21 (1013D).

AELRED. What, for instance? Do you not understand that it is immortal?

JOHN. Although I am bound to believe it, I shall not be satisfied until I understand it.

AELRED. To believe first and then to understand is the rightful order, 'because unless you believe', said the prophet, 'you shall not understand'.* If, however, you recall to mind what was discussed on the nature of the soul, belief will easily cross the borderline into understanding. The first question, therefore, to be asked is: 'What is death?'. And the second is whether the soul incurs or can incur death.

Is 7:9 (LXX).

JOHN. I have no doubt that this is the right order. What, therefore, is death?

AELRED. Trees die, animals die, men die. But that an angel, good or bad, cannot die is clear enough to you.

JOHN. Why cannot angels die?

AELRED. Angels either have bodies that are immortal or they are spirits without bodies. But the soul is a kind of rational life. Life cannot die any more than a light can turn to darkness or a fire can grow cold.*

JOHN. But does not the life of an animal or a tree die?

Bern.SC 81,5 (1173); Aug.Gen. 2,4,6(281); Trin. 5,4,5(913).

AELRED. Certainly. An animal and a tree die through the separation of the elements of its life, but the life itself is said to die from the fact that it ceases to be what it was, which is life.

JOHN. Why should I not say the same about the soul?

AELRED. It is a very different matter. Remember what we said in our first discussion, that the life which belongs to trees and animals is confined to corporeal qualities and that both the movement by which they live and the powers by which they feel arise from very subtle, purified and fluid elements.

JOHN. I remember that perfectly. But what has it to do with the question?

AELRED. A great deal. From it you should understand that the death of a tree or an animal is nothing more than the separation of the life and the body which were joined together, and that the death of both is the breaking up of those elements, which were combined by a suitable degree of heat to create or preserve movement and feeling in the body. Have you any different ideas?

JOHN. No.

*motus

AELRED. Now observe in a living man that movement* by which he grows and the power within that movement by which he feels, and in sense itself the rational soul which distinguishes and which controls both movement and sense. When these are separated from one another, that disintegration or separation of the combined parts constitutes the death of the body. Movement and sense cease to exist, and consequently cease to exist anywhere. But the rational soul, though ceasing to exist in the body, does not cease to exist.

JOHN. One thing I would like to know is, why does the rational soul not cease to exist, when, as you have remarked about the sense, it ceases to exist there?

AELRED. Because, as we have said, sense arises from the combination of very subtle elements. When the dissolution of these elements occurs through failure of the organs, sense ceases to exist. But this is not the case with the soul. Since the soul is life, which is simple, without composition and surpassing the subtlety of all bodily things, it suffers no separation or division. We have stated earlier that since memory, reason and will are one substance and one soul they cannot be separated from one another, for where there is no joining together, there can be no separation, and where there is no separation, there is no death.

JOHN. It seems to me that the soul could fade and die out like a flame in a lamp, which we see gradually growing less and finally going out.

AELRED. Your fantasy is playing tricks with you. In thinking of the soul you have not completely divested yourself of bodily figments but are caught up in certain images. That visible flame by which some things are burned is corporeal and some scholars would hold that it is not an element but a composite body formed from four elements, the fiery element dominating the other three. So since there is combination in it, it is subject to separation. In the case of a pure element, which can be conceived without the admixture of any other elements, as nothing is joined to it, so nothing can be separated from it. But if it is combined with other elements, as occurs in divers substances, then it can be separated from them either actually or notionally or both. The soul, however, is of a totally different kind of subtlety from that of the invisible fire, whose greatest and most subtle power resides in the senses, as we have said earlier, since sense itself is far removed in subtlety from the soul. Consequently, the life of the senses is subject to death because it is subject to division. But rational life, which is without composition and is nothing but rational life, could die only if it ceased to be rational life. Since this life was created without matter and was created only as life, how, then, can it be anything else but life?

JOHN. I would raise some objections that trouble me, were it not that you had clearly shown that reason is a substance. But because I am bound to admit that reason does not reside in the substance of the soul but constitutes the very substance of the soul, I now see how reason cannot die.

AELRED. Take another argument by which you may firmly understand that the soul is immortal.

JOHN. I could wish for nothing more.

AELRED. To what extent does the soul of a beast exert its power on things?

JOHN. I think you have made this clear enough, namely, what it can do in the five senses of the body and what it does by bodily images conveyed through those senses.

AELRED. You have remembered it well. Has the brute soul, therefore, any power over matters which are neither corporeal nor have the shape of bodies?

JOHN. I do not know.

AELRED. How is that? Have you forgotten that we spoke of the theory of numbers as being something great and that the brute soul could not aspire to comprehending it?

JOHN. Your reminder is timely.

AELRED. Listen carefully.[1] A corporeal soul and corporeal images can be divided either actually or notionally, and for this reason appear to be subject to a kind of death. Therefore, since it is mortal, the brute soul cannot possibly enjoy immortality. Furthermore, the principles of all the arts are imperishable, and since the soul from its very nature contains within itself these principles, it can grasp them. If it were not itself imperishable, it could not possibly do this. Otherwise, it would be mortal. Wisdom, which the soul can share, is immortal, but were the soul mortal it could not share it. From these arguments we understand clearly that the soul is immortal. If this seems obscure to you, take it on the authority of many learned men and particularly on the authority of the Catholic faith, which believes that not only our souls but also our bodies will enjoy immortality. Even the pagans believed that angels possessed immortal bodies. For one of them, named Plato, represented God the Father as addressing the gods, whom He had created and whom we call angels, in the following words: 'Since you had a beginning you cannot be immortal nor indissoluble. But you shall not be subject to dissolution, nor shall the fates of death destroy you, nor shall they be more powerful than my will, which is a stronger bond for your

---

1. What follows is a résumé of Augustine's reasoning in *De immortalitate animae* iv (1023-24).

preservation than that which binds you together'.[2] Notice what he said, what he
thought, how much power he attributed to
His will and how much to the design of the
Creator. Because they were created mortal,
which means that they were the combination
of two things, he reminds them that they
could not be imperishable. 'All the same', he
said, 'you shall not be subject to dissolution
nor shall the fates of death destroy you.'
Observe the wonderful subtlety of the man.
He said that they could not be immortal or
subject to dissolution, and yet he appears to
affirm that they will not be dissolved and
perish. The fact is, he distinguishes between
the nature of the creature and the will and
design of the Creator. All those things that are
composite are by their nature subject to dissolution, but through the will and design of
God many things have the privilege of not
being dissolved. Thus, a man and a person
is made up of a body and a rational soul,
which were joined together at the first creation, but though by nature they could be
separated they have, through the goodness of
the Creator, the capability of not being
disjoined. Therefore, if you wish, let us imagine God saying, as it were, to Adam and Eve:
'Since you had a beginning and are the combination of two things, you cannot be immortal and imperishable. If you are obedient,
however, my will shall grant you what you are
denied by your nature. But if you transgress

2. *Timaeus* (ed. Bury, p. 88). The version quoted here by Aelred is
taken from Augustine, *De civitate Dei* 13, 16, 1(388), who was using
Cicero, *De universo.*

my command, you will surely be subject to dissolution, which is nothing less than death.' Man, therefore, can die, because what is joined together can be separated. But the soul, which is not the combination of different things, how can that die? For there can be no separation unless there was a previous combination, and its life, unlike that of the tree or the beast, is not received from elsewhere, but is created simple and subsisting by itself.

JOHN. Did you not say that in the substance of the soul three faculties—reason, memory, and will—came together? Why, then, can they not be separated, since they can be joined together?

AELRED. This question of yours puts me to shame, I must admit. I never said that these three faculties were joined together in the substance of the soul. What I said was that these three are the one substance of the soul, one simple, noncomposite life, which is made to the image of its Creator, who, though He is one God and one Essence, is nevertheless Father, Son and Holy Spirit; and they are three in such a way that there can be no commingling between the three, and no division or separation from their unity. In the same way, memory, reason, and will are three, yet they are one. All our arguments are confirmed by the authority of the Gospel, in which Our Saviour makes this solemn declaration: 'Fear not those who kill the body, but are not able to kill the soul'.* 'They cannot **Mt 10:28* kill the soul', he says. Who are they? The persecutors. Men, therefore, and much less creatures of a lower nature, cannot kill a

*Lk 12:5

soul. Who then? Devils? 'Fear not those who cannot kill the soul', he says. The devils certainly ought to be feared if they can kill the soul. 'But fear him', he added. He did not say 'them' but 'him', 'who, after he has killed the body, has power to send it to perdition'.* If he were speaking of the soul when he said 'after he was killed', he would not have added, 'who has power to send it to perdition'. For if the soul were killed, there would be nothing left to send to perdition. The death of the soul, therefore, consists in being sent to perdition, and such a death cannot be suffered by anything that can die. Note carefully also the error of which Christ proved the Saducees to be guilty. 'The God of Abraham and the God of Isaac and the God of Jacob is not the God of the dead but of the living.'* All those patriarchs were dead, buried in a double cave in the land of Canaan.* Dead certainly in the flesh, but living to God in their souls, for God is God of the living, not of the dead.* Paul wished to be dissolved and to be with Christ,* because only when the flesh was dead could his soul be with Christ.

*Lk 10:37-38

*Gen 23:19-20

*Rom 6:10
*Phil 1:23

Time would run out before I could collect together all the passages from Sacred Scripture that testify to the immortality of the soul, especially since no one argues against this assertion. But many find pleasure in seeking proofs for it and are delighted when they find them. Now, however, if you are amenable, let us restore our energies by silence,* so that when time and place allow, and if you have any questions, we can discuss the departure of the soul and its state after death.

*Greg.Dial.2,38
(134).

END OF BOOK TWO

BOOK THREE

JOHN. I see, as I greatly hoped, that you have some free time.* So, now the silence has been broken, fulfil your promise to give me your views on the departure of the soul from the body and later on reply to my questions about its state after death.

*Aug.Quant.1,1,1 (1035).

AELRED. We shall not have much difficulty with this question, providing you have remembered what was said about the nature of the soul. Before we proceed, then, tell me if you recall how we described the way in which the soul is contained in the body.

JOHN. As you wish. But if I make a mistake, correct me, and when I stumble or flounder, help me along with your word of authority.

AELRED. Certainly I will. All the same, I consider it a pleasure to test your interest and application to the matters you have heard and a satisfaction to see how good your memory is.

JOHN. I accept as sufficiently proven that the soul is incorporeal and immortal. Although, in a manner of speaking, it may be said to exist in a place, yet it cannot be extended or enlarged or confined within any dimensions, that is, length, breadth, or height, nor is it larger in the whole than in the part. It moves the body through space, but itself is not moved in space, as Saint Augustine clearly shows in his book *De Genesi ad*

111

*8,21,42 (389);
8,22,43 (389).

litteram. * Since, therefore, the soul is a simple substance, which can be made neither greater nor smaller, it is of such great subtlety that it surpasses all bodily quality, so much so that although all bodies, according to Saint Augus-

Gen.7,20,26(365). tine,* can be changed into other bodies, the body cannot be changed into a spirit, neither can a spirit be transformed into a body. I remember our discussion about the soul not being held within the body or being mingled with it except by means of some very subtle force which, while not being a spirit, is so close in subtlety to a spirit that it is even called a spirit.

vis sensualis This is the power of sense, which is formed from the very subtle elements of fire and air in a fluid state, which are so purified from the gross matter of bodies that it is able to supply life to certain bodies, or if set on fire or closely compacted, is somehow capable of receiving a rational soul which, so to say, presides over it, rests in it, puts it in order and through it holds sway over the body and the members subject to it.

AELRED. I do not regret my labor which has borne so much fruit. But tell me, have you ever been present at anyone's deathbed?

JOHN. Yes, often.

AELRED. Were you able to see when the person was alive or dead, so that at one moment you could say 'He is still alive', and a few moments later 'He is now dead'?

JOHN. I have not really taken much notice of it. But I remember that those who were sitting at the sick man's side spoke in this way.

AELRED. By what signs do you think they could make this judgment?

JOHN. I would like you to tell me.

AELRED. To put it briefly, by sense, movement,* and breathing. All these are present in a man as long as he is alive. You can say that a man is living as long as you can observe that he is hearing, seeing, smelling, touching or tasting. Where there is sense, neither movement nor breathing can be absent. And when these exist in a body, no one in his right mind would doubt that the rational soul exists there too, even though it is unable to exercise its powers in the bodily members which are rendered useless by disease. For when the members are put out of order, the soul is put out of order also, and when they fail completely the soul, having nothing to hold it in the body, ceases to be in the body.

*motus

JOHN. Explain to me what you mean by movement and breathing.

AELRED. I am speaking of the movement which proceeds from the heart and flows throughout the body by means of the veins, which are called arteries.* By feeling these physicians can judge of the health or sickness of a patient. By breath I mean that which is received and exhaled by the lungs from the surrounding air as the food of life; without it, as everyone knows, man cannot live.* We do not say that these three, which we have in common with the birds and beasts, are the soul, but we accept that the soul cannot abide in the body without them. Everyone agrees that once these three have withdrawn from the body or fail the body, the soul has departed. Not that the soul comes and goes

*Aug.Quant.7,13,
20(362);Mamert,
Stat.1,17(719B).

*Aug.Lib.arb.
2,7,19(1251).

like a body: but when those things, by which
the soul is held in the body, withdraw, then
the soul is said to withdraw. It could also be
said to depart when through the defectiveness
of the bodily members it ceases to vivify or
rule the body.

JOHN. Which of these two alternatives am
I to believe is the more credible: that sense
fails so completely that it ceases to exist, or
that sense moves elsewhere and begins to
exist in another place or as another thing?

AELRED. I want you to give me your
opinion about the body: does it, for instance,
fail to such a degree that it ceases to exist?

JOHN. I would not say so, since the bones
remain for a long time after the flesh has
decayed and been reduced to dust. But of the
power of sense after it has left the body, I
find no trace at all. What happens to it I have
no idea.

AELRED. All bodies are made up of four
elements.* The flesh of man's body belongs
mainly to earth and water. The power of
sense, as we have said, is created from fire, the
power of movement from air. Thus the dead
body, as I think you agree, returns to the
earth from which it was taken and will be
received once more by the soul at the final
resurrection. It must not be thought that the
body will be raised without the power of
sense or with another sense different from the
one it now has. The body of man will rise
with all the perfection and the integrity of its
nature, but its corruption will be destroyed.
The Christian faith holds this as certain. Why,
then, should we not believe that the power of

*Aug.Quant.1,1
(1032).

feeling and movement also returns to the elements from which it was created, and that
together with the body it will be taken up
once more by the soul on the day of judgment?

JOHN. How does the soul behave when it
leaves the body? Where does it go to, where
does it reside, what form or shape does it
have?

AELRED. First of all let us look at the
Gospel. 'Lazarus died', it says, 'and he was
carried by angels into the bosom of Abraham.
The rich man also died, and he was buried in
hell.'* What more do you want? What could 　*Lk 16:22*
be more explicit? We certainly do not believe
that the poor man's body was carried into the
bosom of Abraham or that of the rich man
buried in hell. It is the soul, therefore, that on
leaving the body is received by angels if it is
holy; but if it is wicked, is buried in hell.

JOHN. It is this which greatly interests me.
How is it received by angels, in what form, in
what shape? The soul is by nature so simple
and so subtle that it is not composed of parts
and therefore it cannot be touched nor carried
from place to place.

AELRED. To understand this we shall have
to take a roundabout way. For this reason do
not take it amiss if we repeat some of the
things we have already said, particularly since
the discussion may partly explain other
points.

JOHN. Provided it leads to the desired
conclusion a long argument will not bother
me much.

AELRED. We have spoken of what the soul

can do through the senses, what it can do
without the help of the senses and what it can
do through the memory, through the reason,
and through the will. From this we gather that
in the rational soul there is a sensory power,
an imaginative power, a rational power, and
an intellectual power. Through the sensory
power it perceives colors, sounds, scents,
tastes, hardness, and softness. Through the
imaginative power it mulls over all the forms
and shapes that have been impressed on the
soul by the senses and from them creates
many other images. Further, through the rational power it distinguishes between true and
false. This power embraces many other things
besides, which you will remember having fully
discussed. But through the intellectual power
the soul passes beyond all bodily creatures,
transcends the power of imagination, soars
above all form and shape, and attains simple
and unadulterated truth. Hence Our Lord said
in the Gospel: 'When the Spirit of truth shall
come, He will lead you to all truth'.* Consequently, as long as man lives in the flesh he is
influenced by the bodily senses and during his
waking hours is detached from them but sel-
dom. This occurs, for instance, when he is rapt
in ecstasy or his senses are disturbed by illness
or he is distracted by an alien spirit or his
mind is concentrated in deep thought and
from roving over many topics is bent on one.
Therefore, just as the soul is paying attention
all day to these bodily senses, either seeing,
hearing, tasting, touching or smelling bodily
things, the images of these objects are the
more deeply impressed on the soul and are

*Jn 16:13

with greater difficulty erased. The consequence is that, when the senses are dulled by
sleep, the soul is occupied with the images
that the senses have impressed on it while
awake. No wonder the soul, when reason is
no longer functioning, cannot divest itself of
the images impressed on it, for when the mind
is awake and trying to concentrate, it has difficulty in driving away, even for a single
moment, the frippery of corporeal images and
in attaining a fleeting glimpse of intellectual
purity. *Aug.Conf.7,1,1
(733).

JOHN. Since the soul is naturally concerned with these shapes whilst the body is
asleep, how is it that what is seen has meaning
and that dreams are often prophetic?* *Aug.Cura 10,12
(600).

AELRED. God uses these corporeal images
through the spirits that are subject to him to
punish the wicked and to reward the good, so
that he wisely turns this imaginative power to
the benefit of his friends and to the punishment of the damned. For through it the good
are often enlightened and the wicked
frightened, because secrets are sometimes
unfolded to the former, while the latter are
filled with terror by fearful visions. To Joseph,
under the guise of cattle and ears of grain,
which the king of Egypt saw in his dreams,
was revealed the danger of a forthcoming
famine, preceded by an abundant harvest, and
the way in which he could alleviate such a
calamity was shown to him.* Through cor- *Gen 41:25
poreal images Isaiah saw the Lord sitting on a
high and lofty throne and heard the resound-
ing words that revealed the future blindness
of the Jews.* Daniel, recognizing under the *Is 6:1

shapes of four beasts the secret of the four kingdoms, was told in the words of an angel

*Dan 7:17, 9:22

the time of our redemption.* On the other hand, there is written in the Book of Wisdom this sentence about the enemies of the people of the patriarchs: 'But they who came into the power of night and in their sleep saw a dream coming upon them from the furthest and deepest hell, were sometimes terrified by

*Ws 17:13

the fear of monsters'.* And a little further on: 'Immediately bad dreams disturbed them

*Ws 18:17

and unexpected fears fell upon them'.* And then: 'The visions which perturbed them gave them warning, so that they would not perish without knowing why they suffered such

*Ws 17:19

evils'.* Daniel the prophet also recorded in his book the words of Nebuchadnezzar: 'I, Nebuchadnezzar, was at rest in my house and flourishing in my palace. I had a dream which made me afraid, and the thoughts upon my bed and the visions in my head troubled

*Dan 4:1

me'.* By these examples it is obvious that the imaginative power, in which the soul tarries while the senses are asleep, punishes some and consoles others through the diverse forms of corporeal things.

JOHN. Why is it that the dead often appear to the living, sometimes reproving them, at other times warning them, at times foretelling the future, and at other times earnestly seeking help and making known many things too numerous to mention.

AELRED. Credence should not easily be given to such dreams. Why I say this can be explained in a few words. We have said, as you know, that some people are informed in dreams, some are deceived, some are led into error and others are corrected.* Holy Daniel was enlightened in a dream:† so was Saint Joseph, the foster-father of Our Saviour:* so were the Chaldeans, who were the first mortals to bring gifts to Christ,* and many others. But, as Scripture tells us, dreams have led many into error.* Hence, in his book *De cura agenda pro mortuis,* Saint Augustine says: 'At times men are led into enormous errors by deceitful dreams and it is right that they should suffer for it'.* We read in stories worthy of credence that through imaginary visions some have been deluded by impure spirits, that others have adored demons thinking they were God, that others have defiled themselves with Jewish superstitions, and that others have committed the crime of manslaughter or even parricide. We know on the other hand that good men have been reprimanded and punished in dreams. Saint Jerome recounts that in his dreams he was beaten with rods because he placed more importance on Ciceronian eloquence than on Sacred Scripture.*

The Venerable Bede also, when relating the vision of Saint Fursey, relates that he was accompanied by angels to a terrifying fire. When the holy man showed excessive fear, the angel said: 'Fear not, for you will not feel the heat of the fire you have not yourself kindled'.* When, therefore, he had passed through the fiery smoke unharmed, behold, two of the demons out of the many who were being tormented in that fire, grabbed someone and threw him on to the shoulders of Fursey

*Aug.Cura 13,16 (604).
†Dan 7:1
*Mt 1:20, 2:13, 19:22.

*Mt 2:12.

*Si 34:7

*Aug.Cura 10,12 (600).

*Jer.Eust.30 (416).

*Bede,Hist.eccl. 3,19 (148A).

as he passed by. The angels, returning him to
the flames, said, 'Fursey, the fire that you
have kindled is the one that burns in you'.
The man of God recognized the fellow and
remembered that he had received his cloak
from friends. Because he had died in sin, the
angel showed that his gift should not be
accepted.

JOHN. It seems strange that the soul can
be tormented by an imaginary punishment.

AELRED. Why so? Do you think the
punishment that a man suffers while he is
asleep is imaginary?

JOHN. What else?

AELRED. Is it, therefore, just an image
of pain?

JOHN. I do not know.

AELRED. If that stone were lashed with
whips, cut to pieces with scourges, torn with
spikes or burned with fire, do you think it
would feel any pain?

JOHN. Not at all.

AELRED. So you see that neither burning
fire nor swirling water nor tearing spikes are
in themselves a punishment, but only the pain
which the soul feels from them. And consequently the stripes, with which Saint Jerome
saw himself being beaten, were not a punishment, but the suffering which that frightening
vision inflicted on him was.

JOHN. Since the stripes were not real, how
is it that the pain also was not real?

AELRED. I do not know what unreal pain
is, because if it is pain, it is real pain. If it is
not real pain, then it is no pain at all. For I do
not think that pain can be unreal, unless a

man pretends to be suffering pain when he
feels none, like mourners [at a funeral] who
are hired to show grief for the dead man. Their
sorrow can be called unreal, because while
they feel no grief, they pretend to mourn for
the dead man. For this reason, if Jerome's
soul felt pain because of those stripes, then
he really suffered. And to prove that the pain
which Fursey suffered in his ecstasy or dream
was real, God willed that the burn which his
soul felt on the shoulder should leave traces
on his shoulder as long as he lived. Therefore,
those people who say that a sleeping man cannot suffer torment are voicing an opinion that
is contrary to all human feeling and experience. Having carefully examined these
matters, let us take a look at the question you
proposed about the dead: how they appear
to the living. Take note of what Saint Augustine thought about this: 'Some dead people
are said to have appeared in dreams to the
living and to have pointed out to them where
their bodies lay unburied. But this is no reason for thinking that the dead, who appear to
say or point out these things in dreams, are
aware of them. For the living also often appear in sleep to the living, while they know
nothing of the apparition; it is from those
who have had the dream that they hear of
their having done or said something in a
dream. So, if a person in a dream can see me
pointing out to him an event that has happened or foretelling an event that is about
to happen, while I am completely unaware of
it, and indeed do not care whether he is
dreaming or whether he is awake while I am

sleeping, or whether he is asleep while I am
awake or whether we are both sleeping or
waking at the same time when he dreamt he
saw me, what wonder is it if the dead, quite
unaware and knowing nothing of what is
happening, are seen in dreams by the living
and say something which the living, when
they wake up, recognize as true? I would be
inclined to think that this was done by the
ministry of angels, who receive permission or
commands from on high.' A little further on
he says: 'While I was resident in Milan, a rhetorician at Carthage named Eulogius, who had
been my pupil, told me after my return to
Africa that when he was giving a course to his
students on Cicero's books of rhetoric and he
was preparing a lecture for the following day,
he came upon a difficult passage, and because
he could not understand it, he was almost
sleepless with anxiety. That night I explained
to him in a dream what he failed to understand. Indeed, it was not I but my image, for
I was quite unaware of it and was far across
the sea, doing something else or sleeping, but
certainly not caring about his anxieties. Why
should we not believe that just as a live person sees someone living, so in the same way a
man should see a dead person in a dream,
neither of them knowing or caring who, or
where or when or whose images they are
dreaming about?' Thus Augustine.*

Aug.Cura 11,13 (601).

JOHN. Tell me whether the soul, from the
moment of its departure from the body, can
know what is happening in the world or whether it can appear to whom it wants when it
wants, either in dreams or ecstasy or any other

way? For Saint Augustine relates that when a debt was claimed by a certain man, the promissory note of the dead father being put forward as evidence, but which, unknown to the son, had already been paid, the son began to grieve exceedingly and to wonder how his father, now dead, had not mentioned that he had left debts when his will was made. In a dream the father appeared to the son, anxious as he was, and showed him where lay the receipt which made the promissory note void. When the young man found it and showed it to the creditor, he not only rejected the claim for a fictitious debt but also received his father's indenture. How therefore can it be sustained that the soul of the father had no care for his son? He certainly could not have done so, if he was unaware of what was happening to his son.

AELRED. In the same way that the rhetorician at Carthage did through the image of Augustine, who did not know what was happening to the rhetorician.

JOHN. So, are the saints who have departed to Christ ignorant of what is taking place in the world? And is it a true opinion that affirms the uselessness of appealing for help to the saints, since they are unaware of what we suffer and do not hear our prayers and consequently do not answer them?

AELRED. We are discussing the nature and the natural powers of the soul and what it can do in the ordinary course of nature, not what it can do by permission or command or by the impulse of a superior power. Therefore, when Saint Augustine said that the

spirits of the dead are in a place where they
cannot see what is happening to men in this
world or what they are doing, he was speaking of the ordinary law and course of nature.
Natural limitations are one thing: what can be
done within nature and what outside nature
is quite another. What human nature can do
with the element of water and the element
of fire is understood well enough. Natural
gravity will not allow the human body to walk
on the waves: nevertheless, at the command
of Our Lord Saint Peter set out on his journey
over the water and what was impossible to his
Mt 14:29   nature, he fulfilled by the divine will.* When
the three youths were cast into the fiery fur-
nace, nature yielded up its rights, since either
their flesh grew hard to withstand the heat of
the fire, or the fire grew cold so as not to
Dan 3:23   inflict pain.* Iron, when thrown into a river,
sinks by its natural weight to the bottom: yet
through the merits of Elisha the prophet, an
axe-head rose to the surface and took its place
once more on the shaft from which it had
2 Kg 6:5   fallen.* In all cases, therefore, one must
distinguish between the power and law of
nature and the operations of the divine will.

JOHN. But the rich man who was tormented in hell and was anxious about his
brothers could not have been unaware of their
wickedness, for he was afraid of the torments
they would endure. I would not under any
circumstances attribute this to grace, of which
we judge that condemned man to have been
unworthy.

AELRED. Saint Augustine replies to this:
'His anxiety for the living, although he did not

know what was happening to them, is like our
anxiety for the dead, although we are ignorant of what they are doing. For if we showed
no interest in the dead, we certainly would
not pray to God for them.'*

*Aug.Cura 14,17
(605); Julian,
Prognos.2,24
(486-7).*

JOHN. What then? Was Abraham ignorant
of what was happening in this life?

AELRED. Let Augustine answer this:*
'Isaiah, the prophet, says:"You are our Father,
though Abraham be ignorant of us and Israel
acknowledge us not." '* If such great patriarchs were unaware of what was happening to
the people they had begotten, to that people
which had been promised them as fruit of
their seed because they believed in God, how
can the dead be concerned with knowing and
intervening in the affairs and activities of the
living, especially when some saints, as a great
privilege, have been exempted from human
concerns so that they should not see the evils
which would befall their people? For these
are the words of God to the most holy king
Josiah: 'Behold, I will gather you to your
fathers, and you shall be gathered into your
grave in peace, and your eyes shall not see
the evil that I will bring upon this place and
upon those who dwell in it.'* Furthermore,
when Isaiah reprimanded Hezekiah for having
displayed all his treasures to the Babylonians,
and prophesied that his riches would be carried off to Babylon and that his sons would
be made eunuchs in the royal palace at Babylon, the king, consoling himself that he would
not witness such calamities, said: 'Good is
the word of the Lord which thou hast spoken,
but let there be peace and truth in my days at

*Aug.Cura 14,17
(605).*

Is 63:16

2 Kg 22:20.

*2 Kg 20:16-19.

least.'* The soul of Abraham, therefore, by its own natural power cannot know what is happening here. And if he cannot know, who else can? It seems hard to grant to any of the saints what has been denied to the greatest of prophets.

JOHN. In that case let us surrender to those people who deny that we should pray to the saints in our difficulties, since they are not even allowed to know them.

AELRED. Have no fear. People who talk in that fashion are to be pitied, little knowing what they say or what they are talking about. For, to be brief, although souls cannot of their nature know things which are absent, they can do so in another way. Do we not pray for many people, not only for the dead but also for the living, though whether they are alive or not we do not know? Certainly the saints are aware that the human race is full of misery and as they feel compassion for it, so they most urgently pour out supplications to God. Just listen to the words of him who left nothing untouched, I mean Augustine, whom we take as our chief guide in this work: 'One must admit that the dead are unaware of what is happening here while it is actually happening. But afterwards they hear it from those who, having died, go from us to them and report, not everything, but those matters which are permissible, those that they are allowed to remember and those that the recipients should hear. From the angels also, who are cognizant of what is taking place, the dead can learn what He who governs all judges fit for them to hear.*

Therefore, we do not pray to the saints in vain, since our petitions are made known by the angels not only to God,* but also to the saints, from whom the devotion, faithful prayer, steadfast hope and love of pious souls is not hidden. However, there can be another means, far more sublime, by which the saints, not by nature but by grace, not by their own power but by the great gift of God, can learn of our miseries.

JOHN. Before you explain this way to me, please tell me how one soul speaks to another, and how those who have died lately tell those who have died earlier what is going on in the world.

AELRED. Is the Gospel not enough for you on this point? These are its words: 'And it came to pass that the beggar died and was carried by angels into Abraham's bosom. The rich man also died and was buried in hell. And being in torment he lifted up his eyes and saw Abraham afar off and Lazarus in his bosom. And he cried out and said, "Father Abraham, have mercy on me and send Lazarus that he may dip the tip of his finger in water and cool my tongue." '* That is how one soul speaks to another. 'Father Abraham', he said, 'have mercy on me'.

JOHN. I am extremely surprised that spirits can utter bodily words.

AELRED. You read about eyes, tongue, bosom, and finger, yet you quibble about words?

JOHN. What kind of person was it whose eyes were raised, whose tongue felt pain and

*Aug.Cura 15,18 (605-6).

*Phil 4:6.

*Lk 16:22ff.

who asked for a drop of water on the finger tip? Both of them—the rich man and Lazarus —were dead. Both their bodies were buried; the soul of one was tormented in hell and the other was consoled in the bosom of Abraham. How could one have a finger and the other an eye? Were the members of the body which they used while they were alive, left behind and others created for them which the dead made use of? Or are words being employed in an unusual and eliptic fashion, so that one power of the soul is called an eye, another a finger or a tongue? The words of the Gospel do not allow this interpretation, for it says: 'Send Lazarus that he may dip the tip of his finger in water and cool my tongue.' What power of soul is it that can be burned by fire? Are all these things described allegorically, so that they are not so much a record of fact as a parable?

AELRED. Although Saint Gregory did elicit an allegorical meaning from them,* interpreting the rich man as the people of the Jews and the beggar Lazarus as the Gentiles, we must not believe that the rich man did not really exist, for the evangelist tells us, 'Jesus told his disciples', but did not add 'this parable'. What Our Lord said follows immediately: 'There was a certain rich man.' Just because the same saint, using the same kind of interpretation, equated Simon the leper with the Jews and the sinful woman with the Gentiles, it does not follow that proud Simon did not exist or that the sinful woman did not receive remission of her sins. In Scripture we often find that spirits utter corporeal words.

*Greg.Hom.Ev. 40(1301).

Indeed God himself is said to have spoken on Mount Sinai in the hearing of all the people.* *Ex 19:20.*

JOHN. Well now, tell me how the angel spoke to Joseph in a dream, saying, 'Arise take the child and his mother and flee into Egypt'.* *Mt 2:13.*

AELRED. It is certainly true that the angel said what the evangelist records. And perhaps there were people nearby when Joseph learned it in a dream. Yet what none of the others heard while awake, Joseph alone heard while asleep.

JOHN. How, I ask you, can a sense that is dulled in sleep hear sounds?

AELRED. In the rich man and the beggar all sense was definitely dulled, if not extinct. Yet Abraham heard the rich man crying out, and the rich man heard the patriarch answering. When you are dreaming about a man, you think you are seeing the man. But as soon as you awake and come to your senses you know that you have seen not a man, but his image. If, therefore, he had said something to you in a dream, it would seem to you while you were asleep that you had heard material words through material sounds. But when you wake up, you realize that you have been listening to imaginary words expressed through imaginary sounds. And yet through those imaginary words you have learned something which is not imaginary. Perhaps the words which Joseph heard the angel saying were imaginary, but the fact that Herod was seeking the child to kill him, which he learned from those words, was not imaginary but true. Now that these points have been carefully examined and commended to memory, let us return to the question which you put a short time ago about the departure of the soul, repeating some of the things which were said earlier.

JOHN. The oftener they are repeated the better they are understood and the more firmly are they embedded in the memory.

AELRED. As long as the soul resides in the body, it makes use of bodily members and organs. It uses that vital movement which is common to us and the trees for the growth and nourishment of the body. It uses the sensory movement to make the body sensitive, giving power to the eye for seeing, to the ear for hearing, to the nostrils for smelling, to the palate for tasting, and to the whole body for feeling. It uses the organs from which sense, movement, and memory proceed. I am not speaking of that memory by which we remember and by which we distinguish between past and future, but that memory which has to do with fantasy, which is common to us and the animals and by which animals return to their lairs or their nests and do many other marvellous things. By using these senses the soul receives into itself the images of corporeal things. But just as the soul, when the senses are drowsy with sleep, sees itself in material images and is at one time happily filled with consolation at what it sees, horribly terrified at another or cruelly tormented at yet another, so, when the organs which kept it in the body have ceased to function and it no longer resides in the body, it sees itself forthwith in the image of a body. And in this image it is carried by spirits deputed for the purpose, to be consoled, purged or tormented. This is what the evangelist says, 'It came to pass that the beggar died and was carried by angels into Abraham's bosom. And the rich man died and was buried in hell.' Each of them saw himself in the image of a body, since the rich man mentioned the finger of Lazarus and his own tongue. That he saw the images of other things also which concern refreshment or torment is proved by his mention of water and flame, since he complained that he was tormented by one and asked to be cooled by the other.

JOHN. It surprises me that you call the flame imaginary, for the rich man was buried in hell and no one doubts that the fire of hell is corporeal.

AELRED. We certainly say that the fire of hell, which tormented the bodies of the damned, is corporeal; but whether the souls separated from their bodies are tormented by it is no small problem. Saint Gregory appears to assert that some wicked souls are burned even now by that fire. To Peter, who asked how it was that a spirit could be tormented by corporeal punishment, he replied: 'We say that a spirit is held in the fire, meaning that it suffers fiery torment not from feeling but from seeing it. It suffers the torments of fire from the fact of seeing it, and it is burned because it sees itself being burned. And in this way a corporeal body can burn an incorporeal one while invisible burning and pain arise from visible fire, so that the incorporeal mind is tormented by the flame of corporeal fire.'* These words of the blessed man are

*Greg.Dial.*4,30* (272).*

difficult to understand and there are many who disagree with them. But we must make some effort to fathom the mind of so great a man and, even if we do not succeed, his opinion, though not fully comprehended should be accepted. Now note what he says: 'We say that a spirit is held in the fire, meaning that it undergoes the torments of fire from the fact of seeing it, not from feeling it.' What does he mean by 'seeing but not feeling'? Is sight not one of the senses? How can he see fire and yet not feel it? Since sight is a bodily sense and fire is a bodily thing, how can it see fire and not feel it?

JOHN. In the soul, once it has left the body behind, there is no bodily sense.

AELRED. Note carefully then that he spoke of bodily sense when he said, 'not feeling'. A spirit without a body can have no bodily sense. For this reason he introduces a sense, which is corporeal and a vision, which is incorporeal. Hence there follows: 'It suffers torments of fire from the fact of seeing it, and it is burned because it sees itself being burned'. How does it see itself being burned? By what kind of vision?

JOHN. Perhaps by the same kind by which the rich man saw Lazarus.

AELRED. We are talking of corporeal fire, the fire of hell, in which Saint Gregory said that not only the bodies of the damned, but also the bodies of the wicked are tormented after the final judgement. Concerning the fire in which the rich man was tormented, you know what Saint Augustine said: 'How will the spirits of the wicked suffer in that corporeal fire except, as learned men surmise, because the demons possess some kind of bodies made from dense and moist air, the buffets of which can be felt when the wind is blowing. This type of element would not boil when it is heated up in the baths, were it not affected by fire. If, however, someone should declare that demons have no bodies, there is no need to labor the question. For, why should we not say that in some marvellous but real way even incorporeal spirits can be afflicted with the pain of corporeal fire, if the spirits of men, which are definitely incorporeal, can be confined within corporeal members.' And, a little later: 'I would be inclined to say that spirits without bodies will burn in the same way as the rich man in hell, when he said, "I am tormented in this fire", except that I perceive the answer to be that the flame was the same as the eyes which he raised to see Lazarus, and the same as the tongue on which he wanted a drop of water to be placed and the same as Lazarus' finger by which it was to be done. And yet their souls had no bodies. Therefore, the flame that burned him and the water for which he asked, though having the likeness of bodies, were incorporeal just like the dreams of those people who sleep or the visions of those who see bodily shapes in ecstasy. For even a man, caught up in such visions not by the body but by the spirit, sees himself so like his own body that he cannot distinguish between them.'*

*Aug,Civ.Dei 21,10,1(725).

And so Saint Augustine affirms that the fire in which the rich man was burning was an incorporeal fire bearing a similarity to real

fire, and in this not the body but the spirit
in the likeness of a body was tormented. But
on the question of whether the soul is tormented, or how it is tormented by real fire
before the final judgement, I cannot ever
recall finding anything in Augustine.

JOHN. I recognize the passage from Augustine which you have quoted. He certainly
affirmed that a spirit can be tormented in the
corporeal fire of hell. He also described the
way in which it could be done, when he said:
'Although the demons are incorporeal spirits,
they will be drawn irresistibly to corporeal
fires and be tormented. In some indescribable
way they are inseparable from them, not
feeling the fires, but accepting punishment
from them.'*

AELRED. Perhaps that irresistible attrac-
tion is nothing more than sight, of which
Saint Gregory speaks: 'The torment of fire
consists not in feeling it, but in seeing it', that
is to say, being drawn irresistibly to it, but
not experiencing it corporeally.

And so, take note of the opinions of these
holy men, and remember Saint Augustine's
view that incorporeal spirits can be tormented
in the fire of hell, which is corporeal. Recall
also Saint Gregory's confirmation that the
souls of the wicked are condemned even before the final judgement to suffer in that fire.
And do not forget what Saint Augustine said
about the flame in which the rich man, in the
likeness of his body, was tormented: that just
like the eyes which he lifted towards Lazarus,
and the tongue on which he asked for the
drop of water to be placed, and the finger of

Lazarus by which he pleaded to be cooled, it
was incorporeal. But above all, accept the
words of the Gospel, and with the eyes of
faith gaze upon Lazarus in the likeness of his
body being consoled. If you earnestly direct
your mind to these points, you will receive
great enlightenment in understanding the state
of souls after death.

When souls have departed from the body
and are divested of all corporeal matter and
sense, they are involved with the images of
bodily objects which sense impressed on them
while they were active. In these images some
souls are taken up by spirits of another
nature to be tormented—as Saint Gregory
believes—by the corporeal fires of hell, while
others, in the likenesses of their bodies, are to
be tormented in incorporeal flames—as the
Gospel relates of the rich man. Others still,
according to Christian belief, are purified by
diverse pains and sorrows.

JOHN. I would like to know whether the
punishments of purgatory are corporeal or
incorporeal.

AELRED. I think they are incorporeal,
like the flame we have been speaking of. Some
have considered that this flame was purgatorial. But if it was purgatorial, it was so either
to the rich man or to some other. But that it
was purgatorial for him who was buried in
hell no authority upholds. What is the purpose of the flame then? Either that souls may
be cleansed in it or that they may be tormented in the flame until such time as they
are finally despatched into eternal fire. There
are other purgatorial punishments—such as

fear, sorrow, and horror—by which souls are cleansed. But just as souls endure them in the likeness of their bodies, so also they conceive them in the likeness of corporeal things, as we have shown above in the case of the rich man. For even the philosophers say that after death there are purgatorial punishments, as that line of Vergil witnesses: 'Hence', (that is, with their dying members) 'they fear, desire, rejoice, and are sad.'* This, however, is part of the misery of life. What about afterwards? Is everything all pleasure? Far from it, he says. 'When life departs and darkness closes in it does not leave behind all the troubles of life. Not all ill-fortune or all bodily woes are completely discarded by wretched me'—that is to say, not all the ills that the soul has contracted from the body will be absolutely blotted out. What then? 'Many ills', he says, 'which have grown inveterate over a long period must necessarily remain.' And then he details the punishments by which he thinks the soul must be cleansed from the defects it has contracted from the body, saying: 'They are harassed by punishments and pay the price for old crimes by suffering: some hang naked to the winds for all to see, while others expiate their crimes in the bottomless pit and are burned by fire.'*

*Vergil, Aen.6,733 (242).

*Ibid.(735-9).

These punishments, if indeed they are felt after death, no one would consider corporeal, but as they see themselves in bodily guise, so they are punished in the guise of bodily torments. Now let us hear what Saint Augustine thought about the pains of purgatory: 'Some undergo temporal punishment in this life, others only after death, others still both

now and then. Nevertheless, even before that
rigorous and final judgement they suffer punishment. Who can tell with how many woes
mortal men are afflicted in this life? To those
who are induced by them to correct their
ways these sufferings are purgatorial, but
those who grow worse in spite of such
scourges are cast into eternal torment.'* *Aug.Civ.Dei. 21,*
 13(728).

JOHN. I would like to know whether these
punishments affect souls other than those
which have to be cleansed.

AELRED. On this point Saint Augustine
says: 'Not all those who suffer temporal
punishment after death will undergo the
eternal punishment which follows the final
judgement. For, as we have already said, to
those whose punishment has not been remitted in this life, it will be remitted in the
after life, that is to say, they will not suffer
eternal punishment in the world to come.'* *Ibid.
By saying that not all who undergo temporal
punishment after death will suffer eternal
punishment, he points out that some who
undergo temporal punishment after death
will be cast into everlasting punishment after
the final judgement, while others, who have
been cleansed by temporal sufferings will be
transferred to better things. To all, however,
punishment will be apportioned according to
individual deserts and the decree of the universal judge. Saint Gregory recalls the vision
of a certain soldier, who said that he saw
someone bound in iron fetters who fell from a
bridge, and that while the denizens of a fearsome pit were trying to drag him downwards
by the legs, other men clad in shining

garments were pulling him up by his arms. On the banks of the river stood some dwellings, but the stench that arose from the fetid water and hung about them made approach to some of them impossible.* The sufferings of this life are meted out to each individual according to divine providence, either for the punishment of the wicked, for the correction of the weak, or for the praise and glory of the perfect. For the punishment of the wicked, as in the case of Pharaoh,* who being adjudged deserving of everlasting flames was spared for a short time in this world and allowed to illtreat the people of God, in order that in him God should manifest his wrath and make known his power.*

Greg.Dial.4,37 (287).

Ex 9:16

Rom 9:22

JOHN. Some accuse God of cruelty because, according to the Apostle, God raised him up for the purpose of displaying His wrath.

AELRED. Now pay careful attention. Imagine a king to have condemned someone who has been guilty of lesé majesté, to the flames (which you are to think of as being everlasting), and the day has arrived on which he is to be cast into them. If, therefore, the king defers to another occasion the punishment already prepared and in the meantime subjects him to lighter penalties, would you think him cruel?

JOHN. Not at all.

AELRED. Listen. The time had come when Pharaoh, in accordance with his deserts, was to be thrust into the eternal fire prepared by the devil and his angels. But God deferred this gravest of all punishments, in order that by certain lighter penalties which others could witness, he could display his anger in Pharaoh and the riches of his glory in the recipients of his mercy. It was for this purpose that I believe the Apostle said: 'What if God, willing to show his wrath and to make his power known, endured with great tolerance the object of his wrath, fit only for destruction, in order that he might make known the abundance of his glory in the recipients of his mercy?'.* O my God, what is this I glimpse,   *Ibid. What secret? How fearsome a thing it is to gaze upon, and how terrifying to think about. Stand before your gaze the recipients of wrath on one side and the recipients of mercy on the other. Who could be happier than the one group or more wretched than the other? Woe to them to whom everything turns out for the worse. Happy are they for whom everything turns out for the best. Why, people inquire, did God create men who he knew would be condemned? Paul answers them: 'What, if God, willing to show his wrath and to make known his power, his wrath in the recipients of his wrath, and his power in the recipients of his mercy, tolerated the objects of his wrath, fit only for destruction?' The recipients of wrath are the reprobate. Truly are they vessels fit for destruction, prepared as they were by the corruption of original sin for damnation, for with justice they could have been condemned straightaway. Why, then, did they not perish at that time? Because God endured them with great tolerance. What was the use of that? To make known his abounding glory in the recipients of mercy, that is, the elect. That is the reason why the wicked are created, why they are tolerated, why they prosper, why they are allowed to grow and trample on others, why they are allowed to begin a good work but never to finish it, why they are allowed to mingle with the good but never to stay with them: namely, that God may display the riches of his glory in the recipients of his mercy. Most wretched are they who are neither born, nor live, nor exist, nor even die for their own good, but all that they are, all that they do, all that happens to them redounds to their ruin, while to others all conspires together for their good.*

Rom 8:28, Cf. Aug.Contra Jul. 1,38(1064).

JOHN. Fear and trembling have fallen upon me and dark shadows have encompassed me,* for I know not whether I am worthy of love or hatred.*

Ps 55:5.
Qo 9:1.

AELRED. And so you should tremble, since Paul says: 'I chastise my body and bring it into subjection lest, when I have preached to others, I myself should become an outcast.'* And further on: 'Be not high-minded, but fear. For if he has not spared the natural branches of the tree, take care lest he not spare you.'*

1 Cor 9:27.

Rom 11:20.

JOHN. This is a fearful place.* Let us get away and pass on to more pleasant themes.

Gen 28:17.

AELRED. Listen to Paul: 'The foundation of God stands secure, having this seal upon it: "The Lord knows them that are His".'* These are the recipients of his mercy, whom God has prepared for glory, having chosen them before the foundation of the world* to be holy and without blemish. How

1 Tim 2:19.

Eph 1:4.

wretched are those others, and how happy
those for whom all conspires to their good.
Blessed are they whose sins have been forgiven and whose faults have been glossed
over.* Happy are they to whom the Lord has   *Ps 32:1.*
imputed no wrong-doing. Who could be happier than they whose sins have either been
forgiven or glossed over or not imputed? How
immense, O Lord, is your loving kindness,
particularly for those whose good deeds you
accept, whose evil deeds you pretend not to
see and whose faults redound to their good.
I think it was for this reason that Saint John
said: 'Whoever is born of God does not commit sin'—and a little further on—'And he
cannot sin, because the seed of God remains
in him.'* Who is the man who can be said   *1 Jn 3:9.*
to be born of God? If you reply that it is he
who is born of water and the Holy Spirit by a
spiritual regeneration, then both the elect and
the reprobate are born of God in the same
way. How then are they not able to commit
sin? It is here, perhaps, in this point where lies
concealed that immensity of God's loving
kindness which he has laid up for those who
fear him. Let us act, then, as far as we are
able, in such a way that perfect love may cast
out fear,* and afterwards, perhaps, he will   *1 Jn 4:8.*
reveal it to us. Let us take to heart, however,
the parable of the wheat and the cockle.
Understand by those whom he calls the children
of the kingdom, those who have been
sown by him and are born, as it were, of him
and who for that reason are said not to be
able to sin, because whatever they have done
they cannot perish, for God has made all

things conspire to their good.

JOHN. What you say reassures me. But because you have said enough about the punishments of purgatory, let us now look at the various consolations which the saints enjoy after death.

AELRED. When Peter asked whether the souls of the saints could be received in heaven before they were reunited with their bodies, Saint Gregory replied: 'We can neither affirm nor deny this about all the just, for the souls of some of the just are witheld from the kingdom of heaven and placed apart in certain mansions.'* These mansions are thus described in the vision mentioned before. 'There were lovely green swards sparkling with sweet-scented flowers, on which were seen the dwellings where the men in white assembled, and so great was the fragrance in that place that those who dwelt there or passed by were cloyed by it. Each of the dwellings there was saturated with light.'*

JOHN. Of what nature was that lovely place, the dwellings, the fragrance and the flowers? I can hardly believe that they were corporeal.

AELRED. You are quite right. The finger of Lazarus and the bosom of Abraham were all incorporeal, but they had the likeness of bodies.

JOHN. What do you think? Are consolations given them of a kind different from those which bear a bodily likeness?

AELRED. Many, surely, as far as I can judge. For since Christ grants spiritual consolations to those who live uprightly and well

Greg.Dial.4,26 (263).

Ibid.37(287).

although not perfectly, I think he grants them in greater measure to souls detached from their bodies, either in spiritual sweetness or converse with angelic spirits or in revelation of secrets or in the infusion of knowledge and other matters of this nature, which spiritual people understand better than I do. And perhaps those who have made good use of corporeal things have their consolation in corporeal images full of goodness and sweetness, whilst those who have turned their backs on corporeal things to concentrate on spiritual matters and fill their soul with heavenly experiences will deserve to be more fully consoled with spiritual things. To each one is given grace according to the measure of the giving of Christ. However, I propose this more as my opinion than as my conviction.

JOHN. But Saint Gregory says that the souls of some perfect people are received into heaven immediately after death.* *Ibid.26(263).

AELRED. That is true. But as we have said nothing so far about the perfect, let us look into the matter straightaway.

JOHN. Most desirably.

AELRED. You remember our arguments against the wrongheadedness of those who try to deny the usefulness of prayers and petitions to the saints by saying that the saints on high pay no attention to our prayers and neither hear nor listen to them because they know and care nothing about us. They are encouraged in this attitude because Saint Augustine, when speaking about the nature of the soul, says that when it is detached from the body, it knows nothing of what happens to us.* You must realize that Saint Augustine *Aug.Cura 14,18 (605).

was speaking of what the soul can do according to its nature, not of what it can do by grace. For he says that the soul can know a great deal of what is happening here either through other souls that come from the earth or through the angels, who pass frequently between us and them. But departed souls are allowed to know only those matters that divine providence permits. Be assured that this applies to less perfect souls.

JOHN. What are you saying? Whose soul could be more perfect than that of Abraham? And yet Augustine says that it was from the mouth of Lazarus that Abraham learned of Lazarus' poverty, the rich man's affluence, Lazarus' longing and the rich man's contempt.*

*Ibid.*19(606)*.

AELRED. You forget that at that time the saints were still detained in hell, though far from the torments and the company of the wicked. They lacked, therefore a great deal for perfection. Entrance into the kingdom of heaven was forbidden them and the vision of God, which is the highest bliss of the saints, was denied.*

*Aug.*Civ.Dei.
20,15(681).

JOHN. That is true. Proceed with what you have begun about the departure of perfect souls.

AELRED. We have said that as soon as some souls depart from the body they see themselves in the likeness of their bodies and experience punishment or consolation in places akin to corporeal places. But once the perfect soul, which lacks no perfection—such as that of a martyr—unloads the burden of its body, it finds itself outside corporeal limits, perhaps beyond the limits of all bodily forms and likeness, and in the Creator himself. It has no need of any creature either to travel from west to east or from earth to heaven, for wherever it is, it is, without a shadow of doubt, in him who fills heaven and earth with his luminous vision, his blissful love, his blessed eternity.

JOHN. Are some souls not more perfect than others, or are they all equal in one perfection?

AELRED. Why did you think of asking this question? Did Our Lord not say: 'In the house of my Father there are many mansions'?*—thus distinguishing even between the perfect by a difference of degrees. *Jn 14:2

JOHN. How can anyone be perfect if another is considered more perfect? It is accepted that anyone who lacks something is not perfect. Whatever one is deficient in is possessed more fully by another.

AELRED. You know that as between the saints there are distinctions of merit,* so there are distinctions of rewards, according to the text we have quoted: 'In the house of my father there are many mansions'. One mansion, therefore, is the angels' bliss, another is the archangels' dignity. This must also be understood of the thrones, dominations, principalities, powers, virtues, cherubim and seraphim. These are the mansions from which fell that wretched multitude which did not preserve its due rank and accordingly lost its dwelling place. To restore this ruin God in his compassion put forward a plan as marvellous as it was powerful. For how could he make a *Aug.Joan.67,2 (1812).

greater show of power than by bringing flesh to that place from which the spirits had fallen, and by finding a place for man in the heavens while the angels went plunging down to hell?

Each mansion has its own perfection. Therefore, a perfect man is said to be one who, from all points of view, is prepared for that mansion to which he has been predestined. Hence Our Lord says: 'I go to prepare a place for you',* which as Saint Augustine says,† is nothing else but to prepare the dwellers for their dwelling places. Therefore, all will be equal in regard to eternity, but unequal as regards their mansions. However, they will enjoy equal bliss, because as one love operates in all, each will have what all have, and all will have what each has. But that state of perfection will come about only when this corruptible body has put on incorruption and this mortal body has put on immortality.* In the meantime, either the living are tested in this life, or the dead are released from their attachment to sin, or the less perfect, awaiting the redemption of their bodies, are consoled in their particular mansions. The living stand in need of our wise counsel, while the others by our prayers and the holy sacrifice of the altar or by almsgiving and the chanting of psalms have their glory increased or their sufferings diminished. Those, however, who are in all things perfect according to the state of souls after death, have no need of our care: it is they who plead for us.

JOHN. At this juncture, those of whom we were speaking a little while ago interpose an objection and say, 'How can they possibly

*Jn 14:2.
†Aug.Joan.68,1,2 (1814).

*1 Cor 15:53

help us, since they can neither see nor hear nor know what is happening to us?'

AELRED. Now let these objectors, corrupt in mind, feigning in faith, knowing nothing of the matters they claim to know, come forward. They will not deny that the souls of the saints are received into heaven after death and enjoy the vision of God. If they do deny it, then may there crush them that stone cut without hands from the mountain,* of which *Dan 2:34.* he said: 'Wherever the body is, there shall the vultures be gathered together.'* So you will *Lk 17:37.* not deny that Peter is with Christ, nor will you believe that Paul was denied what we know he ardently desired, to be dissolved and to be with Christ.* But God forbid that any- *Phil 1:23.* one should believe them to be with Christ and not enjoy the vision of Christ, for the highest bliss of the saints is to gaze on that sweet countenance. Let us now listen to Saint Gregory, who replied to Peter, when he asked how Saint Benedict could have seen the whole world in one sunbeam: 'Hold firmly in your mind, Peter, the fact that to anyone gazing upon the Creator the whole of creation becomes petty. No matter how little he sees of the Creator's light, everything created becomes small and the breadth of the mind is expanded by the light of that vision and is enlarged to such an extent in God that it stands far above the world'. And a little further on: 'Why should it be surprising that he saw the world gathered together before his eyes if, being raised above in the light of his mind, he was outside the world?' And lest anyone should think that he saw, not the world but some image of it, as if he were looking at a small picture of some large city, that wisest of men, eliminating such a misapprehension, added: 'When it says that the whole world was presented to his eyes, it does not mean that the heavens and the earth were contracted, but that the mind of the one who saw it, being rapt in God, was enlarged and could see everything that is beneath God.'*

*Greg.Dial.2,35
(130); cf. Bern.
Div.19,3(590);
Aug.Serm.280,5
& 318,5-6
(1283,1453-4).

You see how brilliantly the man of prudence refutes the error of those empty chatterers who in their foul-mouthed drivel say that the saints who are reigning with Christ neither hear those who pray nor are able to offer us any consolation. First of all he asserts that a man clothed in a mortal body has seen the whole world enclosed in one sunbeam. And to his inquirer, seeking a reason for this, he answers that it lies within the power of the Creator, because to anyone gazing on the Creator the whole of creation seems petty. And enlarging on this more fully and proving it more clearly, he says that to him who sees with even a little of the Creator's light, every created thing looks puny. For this reason, if it were possible for a man still weighed down by the weakness of his body to be suffused with such great light of heavenly secrets that in it the whole world should appear so limited as to be seen enclosed, as it were, in one sunbeam, what could possibly escape the gaze of those souls who enjoy in their vision of God that immensity of divine light? It is in that light that they see us, for in it we live and move and have our being.* In that light they hear us, they take note

*Ac 17:28

of what we desire, look at what we need and are present when the holy angels make our prayers known to the Lord.

Therefore, we should honor, praise, and glorify the saints with all possible devotion. We should contemplate their bliss, as far as lies within our power, imitate their behaviour and desire their company. For surely they have a care for us and they pray for us all the more devoutly in proportion as they realize that their own supreme happiness is unattainable without us.

SELECTED BIBLIOGRAPHY

A bibliography of the works of Aelred of Rievaulx, may be found in Anselm Hoste, *Bibliotheca Aelrediana, Instrumenta Patristica 2* (Steenbruge–The Hague, 1962), and 'A Supplement to the Bibliotheca Aelrediana' *Citeaux* (1967) 402-407. H. Silvestre, 'Un répertoire bibliographique pour Aelred de Rievaulx,' *Scriptorium* 18 (1964) 83-85.

For the Life of Aelred, see *Walter Daniel's Life of Ailred of Rievaulx,* edited and translated by F. M. Powicke. Oxford Mediaeval Texts, Oxford: Clarendon Press, 1950. Rpt. 1978, and Aelred Squire, *Aelred of Rievaulx. A Study.* London: S.P.C.K., 1969–Kalamazoo, Cistercian Publications, 1981.

The Dialogue on The Soul

The Latin edition on which this translation is based was made from the four surviving manuscripts of the *De anima.*

Cambridge, Pembroke College, MS 205, 1^r-62^r (seventeenth century).

Durham Cathedral, MS B IV 25, f. 82^v-128^v (dated c. 1200).

London, British Museum MS Lansdowne 209, f. 2^r-31^r (seventeenth century).

Oxford, Bodleian Library MS E Mus. 224, f. 2-62 (c. 1200).

The critical edition was made by C. H. Talbot, and published in *Aelred of Rievaulx: De Anima, Mediaeval and Renaissance Studies,* Supplement 1. London: The Warburg Institute, 1952; and *Aelredi Rievallensis Opera Omnia I: Opera Ascetica, Corpus Christianorum, Continuatio Medievalis,* 1. Steenbrugge/Turnhout: Brepols, 1971.

Secondary works related to The Dialogue on The Soul:

R. Javelet. 'Psychologie des auteurs spirituels du XIIe siècle', *Revue des sciences religieuses* 33 (1959) 18-64, 97-163, 209-268.

P. Künzle. *Das Verhältnis der Seele zu ihren Potenzen.* Freiburg/ Schweiz, 1956.

B. McGinn, ed. *Three Treatises on Man: A Cistercian Anthropology.* Cistercian Fathers Series, 24. Kalamazoo, 1977.

P. Michaud–Quantin. 'La classification des puissances de l'ame au XIIe

siècle, *Revue de moyen age latin* 5 (1949) 15-34.

————— . 'Une division "augustinienne" des puissances de l'ame au moyen age', *Revue des études augustiniennes* 3 (1957) 235-248.

M. K. Otani, *De anima.* An unpublished thesis of the Universita Cattolica del Sacro Cuore, Milan. 1956.

L. Reypens. 'Ame (son fond, ses puissances, et sa structure d'apres les mystiques)', *Dictionnaire de Spiritualité* 1:441-446. Paris 1932.

G. Webb. 'An Introduction to the Cistercian De anima', Aquinas Paper, 36. London 1961.

ABBREVIATIONS

Marginal notes refer to author, work, and page or column reference in the edition used.

Abel.	Peter Abelard (1079-1142)
Theol.sch.	*Theologia scholarium.* PL 178.
Alcher	Alcher of Clairvaux (d. 1175)
Spir.	*De spiritu et anima.* PL 40.
Alcuin	Alcuin of York (c. 735-804)
An.rat.	*De animae ratione.* PL 101.
Aug.	Augustine of Hippo (354-430)
Civ.Dei	*De civitate Dei.* PL 41.
Conf.	*Confessiones.* PL 32.
Contra Jul.	*Opus imperfectum contra Juliani responsionem.* PL 45.
Corrept.	*De correptione et gratia.* PL 44.
Cura	*De cura pro mortuis gerenda.* PL 40.
Doct.	*De doctrina christiana.* PL 35.
Enarr.	*Enarrationes in Psalmos.* PL 36.
Ep(p).	*Epistola(e).* PL 33.
Epp.Man.	*Contra epistolae Manichaei.* PL 42.
Gen.	*De Genesi ad litteram.* PL 34.
Immort.	*De immortalitate animae.* PL 32.
Joan.	*In evangelium Joannis tractatus.* PL 35.
Lib.arb.	*De libero arbitrio.* PL 32.
Nat.bon.	*De natura-bona contra Manichaeos.* PL 42.
Ord.	*De ordine.* PL 32.
Quant.	*De quantitate animae.* PL 32.
Serm.	*Sermo(nes).* PL 38.
SMM	*De sermo in monte secundum Mattaeum.* PL 34.
Spir.litt.	*De spiritu et littera.* PL 44.
Trin.	*De Trinitate.* PL 42.
Vera	*De vera religione.* PL 34.
Bede	The Venerable Bede (c. 673-735)
Hist.eccl.	*Historia.* PL 95.

Bern.	Bernard, Abbot of Clairvaux (1090-1153)
Conv.	*Sermo de conversione ad clericos.* PL 182.
Div.	*Sermones de diversis.* PL 183.
Gra.	*Liber de gratia et libero arbitrio.* PL 182.
SC	*Sermones in Cantica canticorum.* PL 183.
Boeth.	Boethius (c. 480-524)
Porphy.	*In Porphyrium commentaria.* PL 64.
Cassiod.	Cassiodorus Senator (c. 477-570)
An.	*De anima.* PL 70.
Cicero	Marcus Tullius Cicero (B.C. 106-43)
Off.	*De officiis.* Ed. Otto Plasberg. Leipzig, 1923.
Tusc.	*Disputationes Tusculanae.* Ed. M. Pohlenz, *M. Tulii Ciceronis Scripta,* Vol. 14, fasc. 44. 1923.
Greg.	Gregory the Great (c. 540-604)
Dial.	*Dialogorum libri IV.* Ed. U. Moricca, *Dialogi sancti Gregorii.* Rome, 1924.
Hom.Ev.	*Homilia in Evangelia.* PL 76.
Hugo	Hugh of Rouen (d. 1164)
Dial.	*Dialogi.* PL 192.
Jer.	Jerome (c. 347-420)
Ep(p)	*Epistola(e).* PL 30.
Eust.	*Epistola ad Eustochium (Ep. 22).* PL 22.
Julian	Julian of Toledo (642-690)
Prognos.	*Prognosticon.* PL 96.
Mamert	Claudius Mamertus (d. 474)
Stat.	*De statu animae.* PL 53.
PG	J. P. Migne, *Patrologiae cursus completus, series graeca.* Paris, 1857-66.
PL	J. P. Migne, *Patrologiae cursus completus, series latina.* Paris, 1844-64.
Ps-Denys	Dionysius the Pseudo-Areopagite (c. 500)
Div.nom.	*De divinis nominibus.* PG 3.
Rhaban.	Rhabanus Maurus (d. 856)
An.	*Tractatus de anima.* PL 110.
Seneca	Lucius Annaeus Seneca (B.C. 4–A.D. 65)
Ben.	*De beneficiis.* Ed. C. Hosius, *L. Annaei Senecae Opera quae supersunt,* vol. 1, fasc. 2: De beneficiis libri viii. 1905.
Sent.	*Sententiae*
Ans.	*Sententiae Anselmi.* Pl. Bliemetzrieder, 'Anselms von Laon systematische Sentenzen', *Baeumkers Beiträge*

XVIII, 2-3. Münster im W., 1919.

Band. Magister Bandinus, *Sententiae.* PL 192.

Berol. *Sententiae Berolinenses.* Ed. F. Stegmüller, *Recherches de théologie ancienne et médiévale* 11 (1939) 33-61.

Div.pag. *Sententiae divinae paginae.* Ed. O. Lottin, *Recherches de théologie ancienne et médiévale* 13 (1946) 202-221.

Pull. Robertus Pullus, *Sententiae.* PL 186.

Vergil Publius Vergilius Maro (B.C. 79-19)

Aen. *Aeneid.* Ed. O. Ribbeck, *P. Vergilii Maronis Opera.* 1859. (iterum recensuit, 1894, recognovit 1895).

Eclog. *Eclogues.* Ed. O. Ribbeck.

William William of Saint Thierry (d. 1147/8)

Nat.corp. *De natura corporis et animae.* PL 180.

INDEX

CISTERCIAN PUBLICATIONS INC.

Titles Listing

THE CISTERCIAN·FATHERS SERIES

THE WORKS OF BERNARD OF CLAIRVAUX

THE WORKS OF WILLIAM OF SAINT THIERRY

THE WORKS OF AELRED OF RIEVAULX

THE WORKS OF GILBERT OF HOYLAND

OTHER EARLY CISTERCIAN WRITERS

THE CISTERCIAN STUDIES SERIES

*   out of print